CAKES
to fall in love with

CAKES
to fall in love with

Beautiful cakes for romantic occasions

Makiko Searle

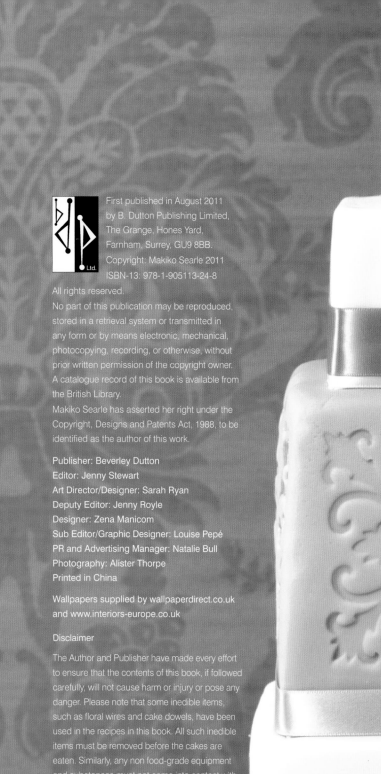

First published in August 2011
by B. Dutton Publishing Limited,
The Grange, Hones Yard,
Farnham, Surrey, GU9 8BB.
Copyright: Makiko Searle 2011
ISBN-13: 978-1-905113-24-8

Publisher: Beverley Dutton
Editor: Jenny Stewart
Art Director/Designer: Sarah Ryan
Deputy Editor: Jenny Royle
Designer: Zena Manicom
Sub Editor/Graphic Designer: Louise Pepé
PR and Advertising Manager: Natalie Bull
Photography: Alister Thorpe
Printed in China

Wallpapers supplied by wallpaperdirect.co.uk
and www.interiors-europe.co.uk

Disclaimer

Acknowledgements

Writing my own book has always been one of
my dreams but I never thought it would happen
so soon. I would like to thank everyone who has
supported me since the beginning.

Thanks to the fabulous Squires Kitchen team! I
am very grateful to Beverley and Robert Dutton
for giving me this opportunity. Huge thanks to the
Editor of my book, Jenny, who has been patient
with me all the way through. As it was a first time
experience, I really appreciated your guidance.
Thanks to the Art Director, Sarah, who took time
and care in designing my beautiful book! I would
also like to thank my photographer, Alister, for
taking the amazing images.

Thank you to my parents, family and my
precious friends who always cheer me up;
my loving parents-in-law, Pauline and Keith,
thank you for helping with my English! Lastly, I
would like to say my biggest thank you to my
patient husband, Nigel, for your support and
encouragement.

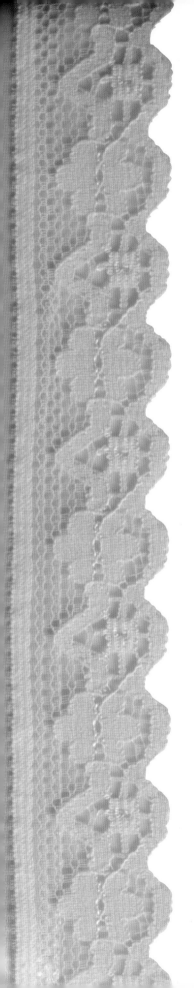

Introduction

When I was a pastry chef, I used to produce all kinds of patisseries. But ever since I started to learn cake decorating, it has always been my favourite subject and given me a great pleasure to create something different and new each time. Having found it so inspiring, I decided to concentrate on cake decorating as the main subject in this, my first book.

When choosing the projects for the book, I carefully selected the cake designs that, from experience, are always popular. Having run my own cake decorating company for a few years, I soon came to know which cakes worked well for a variety of special occasions. My signature 'Temari' cake is one of the most successful wedding designs and it has been made for many happy couples in the past. This is the first time the how-to instructions have been published in a book, so now you can learn how to recreate these cakes in your own kitchen.

Some designs can seem complex, particularly if you are new to cake decorating, but there are step-by-step instructions and photographs for every stage of the process. I have also included alternative methods for creating similar but simpler designs that work well for beginners or those who are short of time. To make things even easier, you can always take just few ideas from each cake instead to create your own, simplified design.

You will need just a few basic skills to make the cakes included in the book, all of which are explained thoroughly in the opening chapters. The projects include many different skills such as sugar flower making, piping, novelty work and techniques that are usually associated with making wedding cakes. I have also introduced some new materials such as rice paper and isomalt for those who are new to the sugarcraft world, so you can try out different ideas to create many interesting effects.

I hope this book inspires you to have fun making wedding and other special occasion cakes. My advice is to always try new ideas and don't be afraid to make mistakes. They can only improve your skills – I have certainly learned a lot from my mistakes!

Maki

Contents

Cake and Filling Recipes

Victoria Sponge

The basic Victoria sponge recipe is simple: all 4 main ingredients – butter, sugar, eggs and flour – are used in equal quantities. You can then add flavouring if required. Sponge cakes can shrink slightly once cooled, so I always make one size larger than required. This also means that you can remove all the crust (see the Preparation on page 26) without making the cake too small.

Round	13cm (5")	15cm (6")	18cm (7")		20cm (8")	23cm (9")	25cm (10")**	28cm (11")	30cm (12")		35cm (14")	
Square		13cm (5")	15cm (6")	18cm (7")	20cm (8")	23cm (9")**	25cm (10")	28cm (11")	30cm (12")		35cm (14")
Butter (room temperature) / Caster sugar / Self-raising flour*	150g (5¼oz) each	200g (7¼oz) each	300g (10½oz) each	350g (12¼oz) each	400g (14¼oz) each	500g (1lb 1½oz) each	700g (1lb 8¾oz) each	850g (1lb 14oz) each	1kg (2lb 3¼oz) each	1.2kg (2lb 10¼oz) each	1.4kg (3lb 1½oz) each	1.6kg (3lb 8½oz) each
Eggs (based on 50g per egg)	3 (150g)	4 (200g)	6 (300g)	7 (350g)	8 (400g)	10 (500g)	14 (700g)	17 (850g)	20 (1kg)	24 (1.2kg)	28 (1.4kg)	32 (1.6kg)
Optional flavours (see opposite)												
Lemons	2	2½	3	3½	4	5	6	8	10	12	14	16
Oranges	1	1½	2	2½	3	4	5	6	8	9	10	12
Vanilla pods	½	¾	1	1½	1¾	2	3	3½	4	5	6	7
Coffee extract	25ml (1½tbsp)	35ml (2tbsp)	45ml (2½tbsp)	55ml (3tbsp)	75ml (4tbsp)	90ml (5tbsp)	110ml (6tbsp)	150ml (8tbsp)	185ml (10tbsp)	220ml (12tbsp)	260ml (14tbsp)	295ml (16tbsp)
Cocoa powder (to replace the same quantity of flour) + melted chocolate	38g (1¼oz)	50g (1¾oz)	75g (2½oz)	88g (3¼oz)	100g (3½oz)	125g (4½oz)	175g (6¼oz)	213g (7½oz)	250g (8¾oz)	300g (10½oz)	350g (12¼oz)	400g (14¼oz)
Baking time	15-20 mins	15-20 mins	20-30 mins	20-30 mins	20-30 mins	30-40 mins	30-45 mins	40-50 mins	40-55 mins	40-55 mins	40-60 mins	40-60 mins
Sugar syrup (see page 10)	80ml (2¾fl oz)	100ml (3½fl oz)	160ml (5½fl oz)	180ml (6¼fl oz)	200ml (7¼fl oz)	250ml (8¾fl oz)	300ml (10½fl oz)	350ml (12¼fl oz)	450ml (15¾fl oz)	550ml (19½fl oz)	700ml (1pt 5¼fl oz)	800ml (1pt 8¾fl oz)

*Reduce the amount of flour by ¼ if you are making a chocolate sponge (see below).

**This recipe can also be used to make 50 small or 15 large spherical shaped cakes.

Optional flavours

Vanilla: add the seeds from the vanilla pods.

Orange: add the zest from the oranges.

Lemon: add the zest from the lemons.

Coffee: add the coffee extract or half and half instant coffee dissolved with hot, boiled water. Heat the coffee and water in the microwave for a few seconds to ensure that the coffee has completely dissolved.

Chocolate: replace ¼ of the self-raising flour with 100% pure cocoa powder; add the same amount of melted dark chocolate with a high cocoa content mixed with an equal amount of water. For example, for a 400g flour recipe, use 300g self-raising flour + 100g cocoa powder, 100ml water and 100g melted chocolate.

Equipment

Mixer

Mixing paddle

Bowls

2 cake tins of the same size (if you have 2, see Top Tip right)

Greaseproof paper

Spatula

Wire rack

Skewer

Preparation

1 Sieve the flour into a bowl. For chocolate sponges, sieve the cocoa powder and flour together.

2 Line the cake tins or baking trays with greaseproof paper (see page 20).

Top Tip

For the best results with this recipe, divide the mixture into 2 cake tins of the same size: this will reduce the baking time compared to 1 large cake and you will find that the sponge comes out much lighter. If you do not have 2 tins the same size, I would recommend that you bake half the mixture at a time.

3 Depending on the recipe you have chosen, melt the chocolate, zest the oranges or lemons, cut the vanilla pods in half and scrape out the seeds, or prepare the instant coffee.

4 Preheat the oven to 180°C/355°F/gas mark 4.

Method

1 Put the softened butter and caster sugar into the mixer with the paddle attachment. Beat on a fast speed until fluffy. Add your choice of flavour (vanilla, lemon, orange, melted chocolate or coffee) at this stage.

2 When the mixture becomes light and fluffy, switch the mixer to a medium speed and add the pre-cracked eggs gradually. If the mixture begins to separate, add a spoonful of flour to help the mixture combine.

3 Add the rest of the flour, gradually folding it into the bowl at a low speed.

4 Using a spatula, scrape off the mix from the side and bottom of the bowl, then mix it through again.

5 Pour the mixture into the prepared cake tins or baking trays and bake in the preheated oven for the required time or until the surface becomes golden brown in colour. When you touch the top of the cake gently it should spring back, or a clean skewer or kitchen knife inserted into the centre should come out clean.

6 Allow the cake to cool in the tin for a while before taking it out of the baking tin. Leave it on a wire rack until the bottom of the sponge is completely cool.

Sugar Syrup

Ingredients

500g (1lb 1½oz) caster sugar

500g (17½fl oz) water

Equipment

Saucepan

Heatproof spoon/spatula

Airtight container

Method

1 Put the ingredients in a saucepan and bring to the boil. Make sure the sugar has melted completely.

2 To store, place in an airtight container and keep in the fridge. It will last up to 3 weeks.

Optional flavours for syrup

Take the syrup out of the fridge when you need it and add your favourite flavour to complement the cake. The following quantities are for 200ml (7¼fl oz) of sugar syrup.

Vanilla: Add the seeds from ½ a vanilla pod.

Lemon: Add the juice from a lemon.

Orange: Add the juice from an orange.

Top Tip

When I make a large quantity of vanilla syrup, I add several empty vanilla pod skins (leftover from baking) as well as seeds. Bring it to the boil again so that you get plenty of aroma from the vanilla pods.

Flavoured buttercream

Green Tea

Orange

Chocolate

Vanilla

Coffee

Lemon

Fillings for Sponge Cakes

The recipes given here are enough for a 25cm (10") round cake. For different shapes and sizes, use the following chart as a guide for the total amount of filling required, based on 4 layers of sponge cake. For vanilla, lemon and orange sponge cakes, I normally fill the cake with 2 layers of buttercream and 1 layer of preserve filling (see pages 14 to 15), so you need roughly two thirds buttercream and one third preserve, e.g. a 25cm (10") round cake would require 1kg of filling made up of 665g buttercream and 335g preserve.

	10cm (4")	13cm (5")	15cm (6")	18cm (7")	20cm (8")	23cm (9")	25cm (10")	28cm (11")	30cm (12")	33cm (13")	35cm (14")
Round	200g (7¼oz)	300g (10½oz)	400g (14¼oz)	550g (1lb 3½oz)	700g (1lb 8¾oz)	850g (1lb 14oz)	1kg (2lb 3¼oz)	1.2kg (2lb 10¼oz)	1.5kg (3lb 5oz)	1.8kg (3lb 15½oz)	2.1kg (4lb 10¼oz)
Square	250g (8¾oz)	350g (12¼oz)	500g (1lb 1½oz)	650g (1lb 7oz)	800g (1lb 12¼oz)	950g (2lb 1½oz)	1.2kg (2lb 10¼oz)	1.35kg (2lb 15½oz)	1.7kg (3lb 12oz)	2kg (4lb 6½oz)	2.3kg (5lb 1¼oz)

Icing buttercream

I use this recipe for stacked cakes as it is very rich and tasty. It requires equal amounts of good quality, unsalted butter and icing sugar. If you prefer a fluffier and lighter icing for cupcakes, use twice the amount of icing sugar to butter.

Ingredients

500g (1lb 1½oz) butter (at room temperature)

500g (1lb 1½oz) icing sugar

Equipment

Mixer with paddle attachment

Makes 1kg (2lb 3¼oz) buttercream

Method

Place the softened butter and icing sugar in a bowl and mix with a paddle attachment at a fast speed until pale and fluffy.

Fondant buttercream

This filling is softer and creamier than buttercream. It requires equal amounts of good quality, unsalted butter and fondant icing sugar.

Ingredients

500g (1lb 1½oz) butter (at room temperature)

500g (1lb 1½oz) fondant icing sugar

Equipment

Mixer with paddle attachment

Makes 1kg (2lb 3¼oz) buttercream

Method

Place the softened butter in a bowl and mix with a paddle attachment at a fast speed. Add the fondant icing sugar little by little and mix until pale and fluffy.

Optional flavours for buttercream

The following flavours can be used for every 1kg (2lb 3¼oz) of buttercream filling.

Chocolate: add 250g (8¾oz) melted chocolate. I recommend using chocolate with over 60% cocoa solids or cocoa mass to get a rich flavour (on all cakes except children's cakes).

Orange: add the zest of 3-4 oranges.

Lemon: add the zest of 4-5 lemons.

Vanilla: add the seeds from 1-2 vanilla pods.

Coffee: add 55ml (3tbsp) coffee extract.

Green tea: add 55ml (3tbsp) green tea extract by mixing 20ml (1tbsp) good quality green tea powder with 35ml (2tbsp) boiled water.

Green tea sponge
cake with green tea
buttercream

Chocolate sponge
cake with chocolate
buttercream

Banana sponge
cake with vanilla
buttercream

Vanilla sponge cake
with raspberry jam and
vanilla buttercream

Orange sponge cake
with orange jam and
orange buttercream

Coffee sponge cake
with coffee buttercream
and walnuts

Carrot sponge
cake with vanilla
buttercream

Lemon sponge cake
with lemon curd and
lemon buttercream

Ganache

This filling is perfect for rich chocolate sponge cakes.

Ingredients

500g (1lb 1½oz) dark chocolate (53-55% cocoa solids)

500g (1lb 1½oz) single cream

120g (4¼oz) glucose

Equipment

Saucepan

Heatproof spoon/spatula

Whisk

Method

1 Bring the cream to the boil in a saucepan and add the glucose.

2 Place the chocolate into a heatproof bowl and pour the cream/glucose mixture over the chocolate. Leave it while the chocolate is melting then gently stir it with a whisk.

3 Allow to cool before using as a filling.

Preserve Fillings

Lemon curd

Ingredients

200g (7¼oz) eggs (approximately 4 medium eggs)

Juice and zest of 4 unwaxed lemons

350g (12¼oz) caster sugar

200g (7¼oz) unsalted butter (at room temperature)

Equipment

Stainless steel bowl

Saucepan

Sieve

Whisk

Sterilized glass jar with lid

Method

1 Place a stainless bowl over a saucepan of simmering water to create a bain-marie.

2 Mix the eggs, lemon juice and sugar together and pass it through a sieve (this is essential for making a smooth texture).

3 Pour the mixture and lemon zest into the bain-marie and whisk together. Allow to thicken (this will take approximately 10 minutes), stirring constantly to stop it from curdling.

4 Once thickened, remove from the heat, add the softened butter and mix it through. If you would like the curd to be completely smooth, pass it through a sieve at this stage to remove the bits of zest.

5 Pour the curd into a sterilized jar and cover immediately to stop it skinning over.

Apple and blackcurrant compote

Ingredients

2 cooking apples

2 Golden Delicious apples

100g (3½oz) sugar

100g (3½oz) blackcurrants

Cinnamon (optional)

Equipment

Sharp knife

Saucepan

Heatproof spoon/spatula

Method

1 Peel and chop up all the apples and put them into a saucepan. Sprinkle the sugar over the apples and mix it through. If you would like to spice it up, add a little cinnamon.

2 Place the pan over a medium heat and stir constantly. The juice will come out gradually, so cook until the apples are mushy then take it off the heat.

Top Tip

If you would like to keep the compote for longer, store the apple compote in a clean, airtight container. This will keep for a few weeks in the fridge.

3 Add fresh blackcurrants to the apple compote. This can be kept for 3 to 5 days in the fridge.

Top Tip

If you store the lemon curd in sterilised jars, it will last for a few weeks in the fridge.

Combining a good quality preserve with the cake filling gives sponge cakes a much richer flavour. Use one that complements the cake, e.g. strawberry or raspberry jam for vanilla sponge, or orange marmalade for orange sponge. My favourite preserve fillings are the lemon curd and apple and blackcurrant compote recipes given here.

Carrot Cake

This recipe makes a 23cm (9") round or a 20cm (8") square cake. For a larger or smaller size, use multiples of the recipe following the table below as a guide.

Round	13cm (5")	15cm (6")	18cm (7")	20cm (8")	23cm (9")	25cm (10")	28cm (11")	30cm (12")	35cm (14")	
Square		13cm (5")	15cm (6")	18cm (7")	20cm (8")	23cm (9")	25cm (10")	28cm (11")	30cm (12")	35cm (14")
Multiple of basic recipe	x 0.3	x 0.4	x 0.5	x 0.7	x 1	x 1.2	x 1.6	x 1.8	x 2.2	x 3
Baking times	30-40 mins	30-40 mins	40-50 mins	40-50 mins	40-60 mins	40-60 mins	1 hour	1 hour	1 hour	1 hour

Ingredients

600g (1lb 5¼oz) dark brown sugar

400g (14¼oz) eggs (approximately 8 eggs)

525g (1lb 2½oz) vegetable oil

540g (1lb 3¼oz) self-raising flour

10ml (½tbsp) cinnamon

5ml (¼tbsp) salt

5ml (¼tbsp) baking soda

400g (14¼oz) grated carrots

100g (3½oz) pecan nuts/walnuts

Equipment

Mixer

Mixing paddle

Bowls

Sieve

Cake tins (2 x same size)

Greaseproof paper

Spatula

Wire rack

Skewer

Grater

Preparation

1 Sieve the dark brown sugar if it has hardened with moisture.

2 Sieve the flour with the baking soda.

3 Line the cake tin or baking trays with greaseproof paper (see page 20).

4 Grate the carrots.

5 Chop the nuts.

6 Preheat the oven to 180°C/355°F/gas mark 4.

Top Tip

If the recipient of the cake has a nut allergy, leave the nuts out of the recipe.

Method

1 Put the eggs, oil and sugar in the bowl and mix them all together with a paddle attachment.

2 Add the dry ingredients into the bowl slowly.

3 Add the grated carrots and chopped nuts to the bowl and mix them through.

4 Pour the mix into the prepared tins and bake it in the preheated oven until the surface is firm to the touch. Insert a clean skewer into the centre: it should come out clean when it is baked.

5 Allow to cool on a wire rack.

Fillings

Vanilla or lemon buttercream filling would be ideal with this recipe (see page 11).

Banana Sponge

This recipe makes a 23cm (9") round or a 20cm (8") square cake. For a larger or smaller size, use multiples of the recipe following the table below as a guide.

Round	13cm (5")	15cm (6")	18cm (7")	20cm (8")	23cm (9")	25cm (10")	28cm (11")	30cm (12")	35cm (14")	
Square		13cm (5")	15cm (6")	18cm (7")	20cm (8")	23cm (9")	25cm (10")	28cm (11")	30cm (12")	35cm (14")
Multiple of basic recipe	x 0.3	x 0.4	x 0.5	x 0.7	x 1	x 1.2	x 1.6	x 1.8	x 2.2	x 3
Baking times	30-40 mins	30-40 mins	40-50 mins	40-50 mins	40-60 mins	40-60 mins	1 hour	1 hour	1 hour	1 hour

Ingredients

225g (8oz) butter

450g (1lb) caster sugar

380g (13½oz) ripe bananas

250g (8¾oz) eggs (approximately 5 eggs)

450g (1lb) plain flour

6ml (1tsp) baking powder

14ml (2tsp) baking soda

200ml (7¼fl oz) water

Equipment

Mixer

Mixing paddle

Bowls

Sieve

2 cake tins

Greaseproof paper

Spatula

Wire rack

Skewer

Preparation

Preheat the oven to 180°C/355°F/gas mark 4. Line the tins with greaseproof paper (see page 20).

Method

1 Cream the butter and sugar together until light and fluffy.

2 Add the well-ripened bananas and mix. Add the pre-cracked eggs slowly. If the mixture begins to curdle, add a spoonful of flour between additions.

3 Add the sieved self-raising flour gradually, in 2 or 3 stages.

4 Dissolve the bicarbonate of soda in the water and add it to the mix.

5 Pour the mix to the prepared tins and bake it in the preheated oven until the surface is firm to the touch. Insert a clean skewer into the centre: it should come out clean when it is baked.

6 Allow to cool on a wire rack.

Top Tip

Bake the cake straight away as the soda will start to activate as soon as it is mixed with water.

Fillings

Vanilla or lemon buttercream filling would be ideal with this recipe (see page 11).

This banana cake is very moist and soft so is suitable for plain shaped cakes (you might find it difficult to use it for shaped novelty cakes). Using very ripe, almost black banana is an important key to the success of this recipe!

Rich Fruit Cake

Bake this cake at 1 to 3 months before you require it to get the best flavour.

Round	13cm (5")	15cm (6")	18cm (7")	20cm (8")	23cm (9")	25cm (10")	28cm (11")	30cm (12")		
Square		13cm (5")	15cm (6")	18cm (7")	20cm (8")	23cm (9")		25cm (10")	28cm (11")	30cm (12")
Currants	120g (4½oz)	130g (4½oz)	180g (6¼oz)	250g (8¾oz)	300g (10½oz)	380g (13½oz)	460g (1lb ¼oz)	560g (1lb 3¾oz)	680g (1lb 8oz)	800g (1lb 12¼oz)
Sultanas Raisins	150g (5¼oz)	160g (5½oz)	230g (8¼oz)	300g (10½oz)	360g (12¾oz)	460g (1lb ¼oz)	580g (1lb 4½oz)	680g (1lb 8oz)	840g (1lb 13½oz)	990g (2lb 3oz)
Cherries	80g (2¾oz)	100g (3½oz)	120g (4½oz)	160g (5½oz)	200g (7¼oz)	250g (8¾oz)	300g (10½oz)	360g (12¾oz)	450g (1lb)	520g (1lb 2¼oz)
Peel	40g (1½oz)	50g (1¾oz)	60g (2¼oz)	80g (2¾oz)	100g (3½oz)	125g (4½oz)	150g (5¼oz)	180g (6¼oz)	225g (8oz)	260g (9¼oz)
Brandy	80ml (2¾fl oz)	100ml (3½fl oz)	120ml (4½fl oz)	160ml (5½fl oz)	200ml (7¼fl oz)	250ml (8¾fl oz)	300ml (10½fl oz)	360ml (12¾fl oz)	450ml (16fl oz)	520ml (18¼fl oz)
Unsalted butter Soft brown sugar Plain flour	120g (4½oz) each	130g (4½oz) each	180g (6¼oz) each	250g (8¾oz) each	300g (10½oz) each	380g (13½oz) each	460g (1lb¼oz) each	560g (1lb 3¾oz) each	680g (1lb 8oz) each	800g (1lb 12¼oz) each
Eggs (based on 50g per egg)	2⅓	2½	3½	5	6	7½	9	11	13½	16
Black treacle	9ml (½tbsp)	10ml (½tbsp)	14ml (¾tbsp)	18ml (1tbsp)	23ml (1¼tbsp)	28ml (1½tbsp)	35ml (2tbsp)	40ml (2¼tbsp)	50ml (2¾tbsp)	60ml (3¼tbsp)
Lemon zest Orange zest	½	¾	1	1½	1¾	2	2½	3	3½	4½
Ground almonds	30g (1oz)	35g (1¼oz)	45g (1½oz)	60g (2¼oz)	75g (2½oz)	90g (3¼oz)	110g (4oz)	140g (5oz)	170g (6oz)	200g (7¼oz)
Salt	2ml (⅓tsp)	2ml (⅓tsp)	3ml (½tsp)	4ml (⅔tsp)	5ml (¾tsp)	6ml (1tsp)	7ml (1tsp)	9ml (1½tsp)	11ml (2tsp)	13ml (2¼tsp)
Mixed spice	4ml (⅔tsp)	5ml (¾tsp)	6ml (1tsp)	8ml (1⅓tsp)	10ml (1⅔tsp)	12ml (2tsp)	14ml (2¼tsp)	18ml (1tbsp)	22ml (1¼tbsp)	26ml (1½tbsp)
Baking time	2½ hours	3 hours	3½ hours	4 hours	4½ hours	4½ hours	5 hours	5½ hours	6 hours	6½ hours

Equipment

Mixer

Mixing paddle

Bowls

Sieve

Cake tins

Greaseproof paper

Pastry brush

Grater

Spatula

Baking paper

String

Thin paper (such as newspaper)

Wire rack

Skewer

Food-grade spray bottle

Tin foil

Preparation

1 Soak the dried fruit in plenty of brandy and a little orange and lemon juice a few hours in advance, preferably overnight. If the fruit is not soft enough, warm it slightly in the microwave until all the fruit has completely softened.

2 Prepare the tins by brushing with a thin layer of melted butter and lining with a double layer of greaseproof paper.

3 Sieve the flour, salt and spice together.

4 Grate the lemon and orange zest. Add the zest and juice into the pre-soaked fruit on the baking day.

5 Just before you start making the cake, preheat the oven to 140°C/285°F/gas mark 1.

Method

1 Cream the butter and sugar together until light and fluffy. Add the black treacle and mix.

2 Add the pre-cracked eggs slowly, mixing between each addition. If the mixture starts to split, add a spoonful of the flour to bind it together.

3 Add the dry ingredients (flour, spice, salt and ground almonds) into the bowl and mix.

4 Add the pre-soaked fruit and zest into the bowl and stir with a spatula.

5 Put the mixture into the prepared cake tins. Tie a sheet of newspaper around the outside of the tin to prevent the sides of the cake from burning.

6 Bake the cake for the suggested time or until it is firm to the touch and a skewer inserted into the centre comes out clean.

7 After you have taken the cake out of the oven, leave it in the tin until it has completely cooled down.

8 Spray brandy over the cake using a spray bottle, wrap it in clean greaseproof paper then wrap it in tin foil to store.

Top Tip

Keep the brandy in the spray bottle so that you can regularly moisten the cake before you decorate it. This method is also more hygienic than using a pastry brush.

Preparing the Cake

The method for preparing a fruit cake for covering is different from sponge cakes. Instead of buttercream and preserve filling, use boiled, sieved apricot jam (glaze) before covering the cake with marzipan.

1 Turn the cake upside down so that the flat, smooth surface is on top. Spray some more brandy over the cake. Fill any small holes or gaps with little pieces of marzipan to create a smooth surface.

2 Gently heat up some apricot jam in saucepan until it is at boiling point (this will kill any bacteria). Spread a thin layer of jam over the fruit cake using a palette knife to provide a sticky surface for the marzipan covering.

3 Cover the cake with marzipan then sugarpaste following the basic instructions on page 26.

Basic Techniques

Lining a Cake Tin

Equipment

Greaseproof paper

Pair of scissors

Food colour pen (or non-toxic pen if you don't have one)

Cake tin

White vegetable fat/butter

Round

1 Cut a square of greaseproof paper a few centimetres bigger than the cake tin.

2 Fold the paper in half then into quarters, then fold it into an isosceles triangle.

3 Turn the tin upside down and place one of the long points of the triangle in the centre of the tin. Hold the paper in place and cut around 1cm from the outside of the tin, using the curve of the tin as a guide.

4 Make 1cm cuts along the curved line to make a fringe, then open out the circle.

5 Lightly grease the inside of the tin (base and sides) with fat or butter and place the circle into the bottom of the tin. (If you have drawn a line on the paper, place this side down so that it doesn't come into contact with the cake.) Check that the paper fits neatly around the edge of the tin.

6 Cut a strip of greaseproof paper big enough to cover the circumference and height of the tin then use this to line the sides.

Top Tip

If you are new to baking, you may find it easier to draw around the tin with an edible or non-toxic pen, cut 1cm around the outside of the outline then snip all the way around the circle up to the line.

Square

1 Place the cake tin in the middle of a sheet of greaseproof paper. Fold the paper up on the left and right sides of the tin, crease and cut to size. The paper should be big enough to cover the base and sides all-in-one.

2 Fold the 2 side pieces in then cut partway up the fold; the cut section should make a square. Repeat on both ends of both sides.

3 Place the greaseproof paper into the tin and fold in the corners. Once you are happy that it is a good fit, remove it, grease the base and sides of the tin then place the paper back into the tin.

4 Trim the paper level with the top of the tin with scissors.

Top Tip

This method ensures that there are no gaps in the lining. However, if you find it easier, you can line the base and sides separately in the same way as for the round tin. Make sure you measure and cut each piece carefully so that the lining is smooth with no gaps.

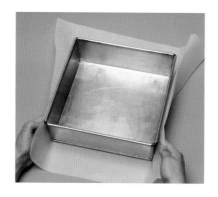
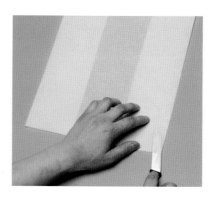

Preparing and Covering a Cake

The cake projects in this book are based on sponge cakes that have been levelled, filled with buttercream and jam then covered with marzipan and sugarpaste (rolled fondant). Creating a smooth, even finish will make your cakes look professional and will give you a good surface for any decoration.

I normally bake the sponge cakes a day in advance (see recipes on pages 8 to 17) and finish all the layering, icing, covering, and assembling on the following day. This way you can save a lot of time and the finish is neater: when you are stacking each cake, you can still smooth out the surface of the sugarpaste while it is soft.

For a wedding cake, I always recommend baking the sponge cakes 2.5cm (1") larger than the size you require as sponge cakes always shrink when baked. You may also wish to remove the crust to achieve a more professional finish which will make the cakes slightly smaller. If you prefer fruit cake, the preparation required is slightly different to sponge cakes. A recipe and preparation method are given on pages 18 to 19.

Cake Covering Quantities

You can use the following chart as a guide to the amount of marzipan and sugarpaste you will need. To allow for the extra paste needed when rolling out, add an extra 50% to the largest cake only, e.g. for a single-tier round 10cm (4") cake you will need 400g + *200g*, or for a 3-tier 10cm, 15cm and 20cm (4", 6" and 8") round cake, you will need 400g, 600g, 850g + *425g*.

	10cm (4")	13cm (5")	15cm (6")	18cm (7")	20cm (8")	23cm (9")	25cm (10")	28cm (11")	30cm (12")	33cm (13")	35cm (14")
Round	400g (14¼oz)	500g (1lb 1½oz)	600g (1lb 5¼oz)	700g (1lb 8¾oz)	850g (1lb 14oz)	1kg (2lb 3¼oz)	1.2kg (2lb 10¼oz)	1.5kg (3lb 5oz)	1.8kg (3lb 15½oz)	2.2kg (4lb 13½oz)	2.5kg (5lb 8¼oz)
Square	500g (1lb 1½oz)	600g (1lb 5¼oz)	700g (1lb 8¾oz)	800g (1lb 12¼oz)	1kg (2lb 3¼oz)	1.2kg (2lb 10¼oz)	1.4kg (3lb 1½oz)	1.7kg (3lb 12oz)	2kg (4lb 6½oz)	2.5kg (5lb 8¼oz)	2.8kg (6lb 2¾oz)

Covering a round cake

The sizes and quantities given here are for a 20cm (8") round cake.

Edibles

23cm (9") round sponge cakes baked in 2 tins

850g (1lb 14oz) buttercream filling

Preserve filling (optional)

200g (7¼oz) sugar syrup

850g (1lb 14oz) marzipan (SK)

850g (1lb 14oz) sugarpaste

Icing sugar for dusting (if necessary)

Equipment

Large, serrated knife

Cake leveller

20cm (8") round cake boards (the same size as the trimmed cake)

Greaseproof paper

Small knife

Large and small palette knives

Pastry brush

Turntable

Side scraper

Large rolling pin

2 marzipan spacers

2 cake smoothers

67cm (2' 3") x 15mm width satin ribbon

Double-sided tape

Scissors

Spirit level

Straight edge

Preparation: Layering and Icing

1 Remove the 2 sponge cakes from the tins (make sure they have cooled completely).

2 Turn one cake over and slice the crust off the bottom with a large, serrated knife.

3 Using the first notch on the cake leveller, slice the sponge from the bottom. Put the sliced side of the sponge on the work surface and slice it again to remove the top crust.

4 Repeat steps 2 and 3 on the other sponge cake so that you have 4 layers of cake exactly the same thickness.

5 Using the 20cm round cake drum as a guide, cut off the crust from the edge of the 4 sliced sponges.

6 Place the cake drum on a sheet of greaseproof paper (this will make it easier to move the cake when it is covered) and place this onto a turntable.

Top Tip

If you find that the cake is sliding around on the paper, put a small piece of non-slip mat under the cake board.

7 Put a tiny amount of buttercream filling onto the cake drum to act as a glue and place the first layer of sponge on the cake board. Brush sugar syrup onto the sponge to keep it moist.

8 Spread a thin layer of buttercream (flavoured as required) over the top of the cake and place the second layer of sponge on top. Brush with syrup again.

9 Spread a thin layer of the preserve filling over the cake and place the third layer of sponge on top. Brush with syrup again.

10 Spread a layer of buttercream on top and place the final, fourth layer of sponge on top. Brush with syrup again.

Top Tip

To check whether the cake is level, place a cake board on top of the cake then place a spirit level onto the board. This is particularly important for stacked cakes.

11 Using a large palette knife, spread an even layer of buttercream over the surface of the cake (top and sides). Level the top with a straight edge and remove any excess from the sides with a scraper.

12 Carefully pull the greaseproof paper to slide the cake off the turntable, then support the cake underneath and place in a refrigerator until firm. Keeping the paper under the board will make it easier to move around until the cake is stacked.

13 Repeat step 11 to make sure the sides are smooth and straight. Chill again until the cake is firm enough for covering, then carefully remove the cake from the fridge and place it onto a non-stick board or work surface.

Top Tip

If the cake is larger than the turntable, use a larger cake drum under the greaseproof paper.

Covering a Cake with Marzipan and Sugarpaste

1 Knead the required amount of marzipan on a non-stick board or on a work surface until smooth and pliable. If the marzipan is a little sticky, use a sprinkling of icing sugar.

2 Use a large rolling pin to roughly measure the cake covering area (i.e. side + top + side). Roll out the paste to the required size, using the 2 marzipan spacers to create an even thickness.

3 Lift the marzipan by loosely folding it over a rolling pin and position it over the cake. Smooth the covering down and around the cake with palm of your hand, pressing gently around the sides to remove any air bubbles.

4 When you have smoothed over the top and sides of the cake, trim away the excess marzipan from around the base of the cake using a small palette knife. Rub the surface gently with cake smoothers to remove all the air bubbles. Trim around the base once again to create a neat edge.

5 Repeat the same method to cover the cake with sugarpaste. If the marzipan is still soft the sugarpaste should stick to it.

Top Tip

I cover the cake with sugarpaste just after the marzipan so it sticks. If the marzipan has firmed and you find that the sugarpaste doesn't stick to it, dampen the marzipan with a little clear spirit (such as vodka or gin) using a pastry brush before applying the sugarpaste.

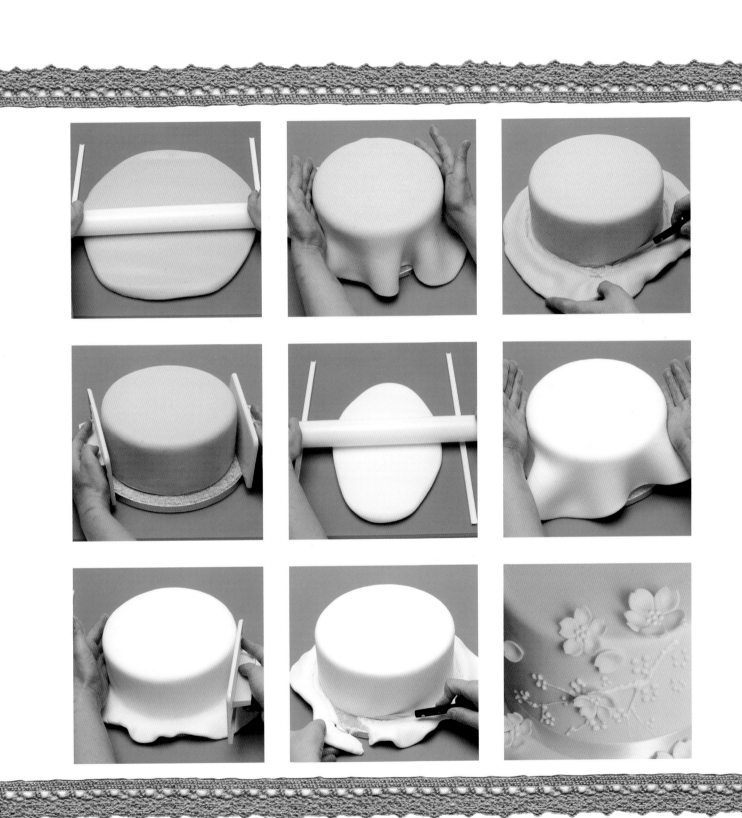

Covering the Base Board

There are a few different ways of covering a cake board but I find the method described here works best for me as it saves time and sugarpaste.

Edibles

Small amount of royal icing

Sugarpaste

Icing sugar for dusting

Equipment

Cake drum, at least 5cm (2") larger than the cake

Non-stick board (optional)

Large rolling pin

Small palette knife

Double-sided tape

15mm width satin ribbon, slightly longer than the circumference of the cake drum

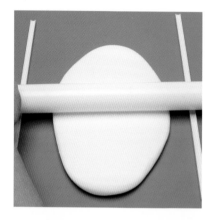 

1 To make a base board for the bottom tier, you will need a cake drum that is larger than the bottom tier. Secure the cake drum that has the cake on top centrally on top of the base board using royal icing before icing the cake.

2 Cover the cake as described on page 26 with marzipan and sugarpaste then cover the base board using the relevant method below.

Round

1 Knead enough sugarpaste to cover the whole cake board on a non-stick board or work surface dusted with icing sugar.

2 Using a large rolling pin, roll out the sugarpaste to an area larger than the cake board. Cut out a circle roughly the same size as the cake in the centre of the paste with small palette knife. The circle doesn't have to be precise so you can do this freehand or make a template from greaseproof paper if preferred.

3 Run your fingertip around the cut edge to make a clean line. Cut through the paste to open up the circle from the centre. Slide this to one side.

4 Place the covered cake and base board in front of you, gently lift the sugarpaste and place it onto the cake board around the cake.

5 Overlap the join then cut through this with a palette knife. Take off the excess sugarpaste and rub over the join with your hand until the creases disappear.

6 Smooth over the paste on the cake board then use a small palette knife to trim away the excess sugarpaste from around the edge. Gently rub the cut edge with your fingers to make it smooth.

7 Stick 2cm-3cm (¾"-1¼") long pieces of double-sided tape at the back and on both sides of the cake board edge, then cover it with 15mm width ribbon. Position the join so that it is at the back of the cake board.

Square

1 Knead enough sugarpaste to cover the whole cake board on a non-stick board or work surface dusted with icing sugar.

2 Using a large rolling pin, roll out the sugarpaste to an area larger than the cake board. Cut the rolled paste into 4 strips: the width of each strip should be slightly wider than the edge of the cake board you are covering.

3 Carefully lift a strip and place it on one side of the cake board. Place the second strip on the second side of the cake board next to the first one so that the ends overlap, then cut through the paste with a small palette knife. Take off the excess paste and gently blend the join with your hand until the surface is smooth.

4 Repeat on all 4 sides and trim away the excess sugarpaste from around the edge. Gently rub the cut edge with your fingers to make it smooth.

5 Stick 2cm-3cm (¾"-1¼") pieces of double-sided tape at the back of the cake board and on all 4 corners then cover the board edge with 15mm width ribbon. Position the join so that it is at the back.

Dowelling and Stacking a Tiered Cake

There are several cakes featured in this book which are stacked. These include everything from the 2-tier Sakura Cherry Blossom cake to the 10-tier Paper Peonies design. Whenever a cake is stacked it is always wise to dowel the tiers (except the top one) to support the weight of the tiers above and therefore prevent the cake from sinking or toppling.

Edibles

Cakes on boards, covered with marzipan and sugarpaste

Food colour pen (SK)

Small amount of royal icing

Equipment

Plastic cake dowels

Dowel template (available from sugarcraft suppliers, see page 118)

Serrated knife

Spare cake board

Spirit level

Ribbon or piping bag with nozzle

1 Using the dowel template as a guide, mark the positions for the 4 dowels on the lower tiers. Make sure the marks are smaller than the size of the next tier.

2 Look at the cake from the side and insert a dowel into the highest part. Mark the dowel just above the level of the sugarpaste covering with a food colour pen. Take it out of the cake and cut it to size with a serrated knife. Use this dowel as a guide to cut the other 3 dowels to exactly the same length.

3 Insert the 4 dowels into the pre-marked positions. Place something flat such as a spare cake board on top of the cake and use a spirit level to make sure all the dowels are the same height.

4 If you are stacking 3 or more tiers, follow the same method to dowel all the cakes except the top one.

5 Spread some royal icing into the centre of the dowelled cake(s), carefully lift the next tier with a large palette knife and position it on top.

6 Once the second tier is placed, use the smoothers to ease the sugarpaste down the sides of the cake to hide the gap between the tiers. Repeat with any further tiers.

7 Attach a length of satin ribbon around the join between the cakes or pipe some royal icing dots to hide the gaps.

Making Mini Square and Round Cakes

Several projects feature mini cakes, either presented on their own or with a larger cake. The Sealed Present Boxes, Material Girls and Bridal Corsages projects are all made using this method. The recipe given here makes 16 x 5cm (2") square or round mini cakes.

Ingredients

18cm (7") square Victoria sponge cake recipe (see page 8)

Edibles

450g (1lb) buttercream filling

180g-200g (6¼oz-7¼oz) preserve filling

200g (7¼oz) sugar syrup

1.12kg (2lb 7¼oz) marzipan (SK), 70g (2½oz) per cake

1.12kg (2lb 7¼oz) sugarpaste, 70g (2½oz) per cake

Icing sugar for dusting (if necessary)

Equipment

23cm (9") square cake tin, lined

Large, serrated knife

Small cake cards or greaseproof paper

Small knife

Large and small palette knives

Pastry brush

Large rolling pin

2 marzipan spacers

2 cake smoothers

5cm (2") round cutter (for round cakes)

Baking the Cakes

Follow the 18cm (7") square Victoria sponge recipe and bake the cake in a 23cm (9") lined square tin.

Covering the Cakes

1 Using a large, serrated knife, slice the top and bottom crust off the cake then slice it into 2 layers. Alternatively, you can use the cake leveller set to the third notch to slice it in half.

2 Brush plenty of sugar syrup over the first layer of sponge and spread a layer of preserve filling and buttercream over the surface. Place the second layer on top and spread a small amount of buttercream over the top to prevent the sponge from drying out. Let it firm in the fridge.

3 Cut the crust off the sides of the cake and cut it into 4 x 4 squares to make 16 x 5cm square mini cakes, or cut out 16 circles with a 5cm round cutter.

4 Spread a thin layer of buttercream over the surface of each mini cake. Place each cake on a small cake card or a small piece of greaseproof paper.

5 Roll out the marzipan on a non-stick board between the 2 spacers. Remove the spacers then roll it out a little more to make the marzipan slightly thinner (the thickness of the covering should be relative to the cake size).

6 Cut the marzipan into squares or circles big enough to cover each cake all-in-one then cover the individual cakes in the same way as for a large cake.

7 Repeat steps 5 and 6 to cover the cakes with sugarpaste.

Mini Cat Cakes (see page 102)

To make the mini cakes for the Cats and Birds project you will need the same edibles and equipment as before. Bake the cake in the same way then use the following method to cover them.

This makes 10-11 mini cakes. Although I made these cakes taller than my usual mini cake size, you can use normal size mini cakes if preferred.

1 Using a large, serrated knife, slice the top and bottom crust off the cake then slice it into 2 layers.

2 Cut out circles from both sponges with a 5cm round cutter. You should be able to get around 33 individual discs from the cakes (you will need 3 discs per cake).

3 Brush some sugar syrup over the first layer of sponge and spread a thin layer of your chosen preserve filling over the surface. Place the second layer on top, brush with sugar syrup, spread over some buttercream filling, and finally place the third layer of sponge on top.

4 Spread some buttercream over the top and sides then allow to firm in the fridge.

5 Roll out some marzipan on a non-stick board, using the spacers to create an even thickness. Remove the spacers then roll out a little more to make the marzipan slightly thinner.

6 Cut the marzipan into smaller pieces (enough to cover the cakes), then cover each individual cake. Trim neatly at the base.

7 Repeat steps 5 and 6 to cover the cakes with sugarpaste.

Working with Royal Icing

There are 3 ways to make royal icing:

1 Use instant mix royal icing powder (the quick and easy method, ideal for beginners);

2 Use fresh egg white (for home baking);

3 Use dried albumen powder (for professional and commercial decorators).

All three methods are described here so choose the one that suits you best.

Basic Equipment

(required for all methods)

Sieve

Electric mixer with paddle attachment

Weighing scales

Spatula

Airtight plastic container

Bowl

Spoon

Clean tea towel

Cling film

Method 1
Instant mix icing

Edibles

500g pack Instant Mix Royal Icing (SK)

75ml (2½fl oz) cooled, boiled water

Method

1 Sift the contents of the pack into a mixing bowl and add 75ml of cooled, boiled water.

2 Using the paddle attachment, mix at a low speed for approximately 5 minutes in a mixer until light and fluffy. The correct consistency has been reached when the icing is whiter and will stand in peaks with the tips bending over (soft-peak consistency).

3 Place in a clean bowl with a clean, damp tea towel on top to stop a crust forming on the icing. If you do not need the icing straight away, place it in a plastic container with a piece of cling film over the top. Make sure the top of the container is completely covered. Place the lid on securely and store at room temperature until required.

Method 2
Fresh egg white

Edibles

90g (3¼oz) free range egg white (from approximately 3 eggs)

455g (1lb) icing sugar

5 drops lemon juice

Method

1 Sift the icing sugar into a mixing bowl. Pass the fresh egg white through a sieve and add it to the sugar.

2 Using the paddle attachment, mix at a low speed for approximately 5 minutes in a mixer until light and fluffy. Add the lemon juice. The correct consistency has been reached when the icing is whiter and will stand in peaks with the tips bending over (soft-peak consistency).

3 Place in a clean bowl with a clean, damp tea towel on top to stop a crust forming on the icing. If you do not need the icing straight away, place it in a plastic container with a piece of cling film over the

top. Make sure the top of the container is completely covered. Place the lid on securely and store at room temperature until required.

If you are using fresh egg white, visit the British Egg Information Service website at www.britegg.co.uk or the Food Standards Agency website at www.food.gov.uk to make sure you are using raw eggs safely.

Method 3

Dried albumen (egg white) powder

Edibles

15g (½oz) pasteurised, dried albumen powder*

85ml (3fl oz) pre-boiled, lukewarm water

455g (1lb) icing sugar

*Follow the instructions for use on the back of the albumen powder you are using as the strength of albumen can differ depending on the product.

Method

1 Mix the powdered albumen and pre-boiled, lukewarm water in a bowl and mix it until the powder until it has completely dissolved.

2 Sift the icing sugar into a mixing bowl. Pass the liquid albumen through a sieve and add it to the sugar.

3 Using the paddle attachment, mix at a low speed for approximately 5 minutes in a mixer until light and fluffy. The correct consistency has been reached when the icing is whiter and will stand in peaks with the tips bending over (soft-peak consistency).

4 Place in a clean bowl with a clean, damp tea towel on top to stop a crust forming on the icing. If you do not need the icing straight away, place it in a plastic container with a piece of cling film over the top. Make sure the top of the container is completely covered. Place the lid on securely and store at room temperature until required.

Consistencies of royal icing

Stiff peak

This consistency is suitable for piping leaves, basket weave effects, and for use between stacked cakes to hold them in place. Add 1 heaped teaspoon of icing sugar to every 90g (3oz) of royal icing and stir. When lifted with a palette knife the icing should form stiff peaks.

If you are piping with stiff-peak icing, you will need to remove some of the air from the icing first. Using a palette knife, take some icing out of the bowl and rub/paddle it back and forth on a clean surface a few times before placing it into a piping bag.

Soft peak

This consistency is suitable for pressure piping onto the sides of cakes and for the outline of run-out pieces and cookies. When lifted with a palette knife the icing should form peaks that bend over at the tip.

Using a palette knife, take some icing out of the bowl and rub it back and forth on a clean surface until it is smooth before placing it into a piping bag.

Run-out

This consistency is suitable for flooding in run-outs, including when decorating cookies.

Place some icing in a bowl, add a little cold water and stir. Cut through the icing with a palette knife: the consistency is correct if it flows together after 10 seconds. If it takes longer, add a little more water.

Top Tip

Even if you are using a soft-peak or run-out consistency royal icing, start by making stiff-peak royal icing first, then you can add cooled, boiled water to adjust the softness of the icing.

Making a piping bag

Equipment

Greaseproof paper

Large, sharp knife

Scissors

Piping nozzle (if required)

Method

1 Take a sheet of greaseproof paper measuring 76cm x 46cm and fold it in half. Using a large, sharp knife, cut the sheet in half. Fold both pieces in half again and cut to make 4 rectangles.

2 Fold the paper on the diagonal but not point-to point, there should be a strip on either side of the triangle. Cut along the fold with a sharp knife.

3 Bring one side of the bag round to create a point in the middle of the long side. Hold this in position then bring the other side round in the same way.

4 Fold in the corners of the bag then make 2 small tears and fold in to hold the bag in place. This will stop the bag from opening.

5a If you are not using a nozzle, half-fill the bag with royal icing. Flatten the top, fold in the corners like an envelope then fold the point twice to secure. Snip off the tip when you are ready to pipe.

5b If you are using a piping nozzle, cut just over 1cm off the end of the bag and place the nozzle inside before half-filling with icing. Flatten the top, fold in the corners like an envelope then fold the point twice to secure.

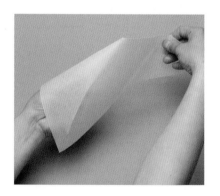

Equipment

Most of the cakes in this book have been made using the same basic equipment, so you won't need to invest in a wide range of items. A full list of equipment is shown here so that you can see what some of the more specialist items look like, but you will find the essential items listed on page 40. Anything that is specific to a cake design is listed at the beginning of the project, as well as all the edibles that you will need.

1 Cake cards, boards and drums
2 Cake dowels
3 Cake leveller
4 Cake tins
5 Cling film
6 Cocktail sticks
7 Cooling rack
8 Craft knife
9 Cupcake cases
10 Cupcake tin
11 Cupcake wrappers
12 Double-sided sticky tape
13 Floristry tape
14 Floristry wires
15 Flower picks
16 Foam pad
17 Food-grade plastic gloves
18 Grater
19 Greaseproof paper
20 Greaseproof piping bags
21 Great Impressions moulds (SK)
22 Kitchen paper
23 Large, non-stick board
24 Large palette knife
25 Large rolling pin

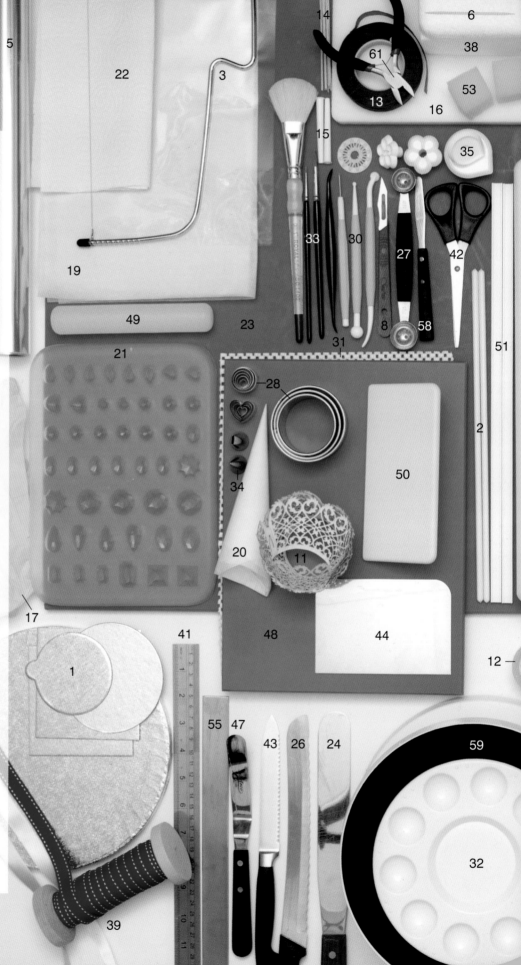

26 Large, serrated knife
27 Melon scoop
28 Metal cutters
29 Mixer
30 Modelling tools: scriber, ball tool, Dresden tool
31 Non-slip mat
32 Paint palette
33 Paintbrushes
34 Piping nozzles
35 Plastic cutters
36 Pastry brush
37 Plastic piping bags
38 Polystyrene dummies
39 Ribbon
40 Rubber spatula
41 Ruler
42 Scissors
43 Sharp knife
44 Side scraper
45 Sieve
46 Silicone rubber half-sphere bakeware
47 Small, cranked palette knife
48 Small, non-stick board
49 Small rolling pin
50 Smoother
51 Spacers
52 Spirit level
53 Sponge pieces
54 Steel or copper saucepan
55 Straight edge
56 Tea towel
57 Thermometer
58 Tiny palette knife (Kemper tool)
59 Turntable
60 Weighing scales
61 Wire cutters

Cake covering essentials

All of the cake projects featured in this book require some basic equipment to prepare and cover the cakes before they are decorated. Full instructions for levelling, filling and covering cakes are given on pages 23 to 27.

Cake cards, boards and drums

Cake leveller

Greaseproof paper

Icing sugar shaker

Large, non-stick board

Large palette knife

Large rolling pin

Large, serrated knife

Non-slip mat

Pastry brush

Scissors

Sharp knife

Side scraper

Smoothers

Spacers

Spirit level

Straight edge

Turntable

Decorating essentials

You only need a few basic items to start cake decorating, some of which you may have in your kitchen already and some of which are available from sugarcraft suppliers (see page 118). I find that I use these items for almost every cake I decorate, so would recommend having them to hand before you start any project. Any additional equipment is listed at the beginning of each project.

Cake dowels (for stacked cakes)

Clear spirit (e.g. vodka or gin) or glaze cleaner (IPA)

Cocktail sticks

Craft knife

Double-sided sticky tape

Edible glue

Foam pad (firm, for thinning petals, etc.)

Greaseproof piping bags

Kitchen paper

Metal cutters

Modelling tools: ball tool, scriber, Dresden tool

Paint palette

Paintbrushes

Piping nozzles

Plastic cutters

Polystyrene dummies

Ribbon

Ruler

Sheet of foam sponge (for drying small pieces)

Small, cranked palette knife

Small, non-stick board

Small rolling pin

Tin foil

Tiny palette knife (Kemper tool)

White vegetable fat

Edibles

A brief description of the icings, pastes and food colourings that you will need is given here. All of the edibles used for the cakes in this book are available from cake decorating suppliers (see page 118); recipes for the cakes themselves and suggested fillings can be found on pages 8 to 19.

Cake fillings

If you are using sponge cake for the base, soak it with sugar syrup to keep it moist and use a creamy filling such as buttercream or chocolate ganache between the layers and as a crumb-coat (to help the marzipan covering stick). If you would like to add extra flavour, you can use a preserve filling such as raspberry jam or lemon curd in conjunction with the cream-based filling. Recipes and flavouring options are given on pages 8 to 19.

Marzipan

Made from ground almonds and sugar, marzipan is a traditional covering used to seal the cake and give it a smooth, professional finish. Always use a good quality marzipan with a high almond content (minimum 23.5%). If you are using sponge cakes you can leave off the marzipan coating but this only applies to mini cakes. To achieve a smooth and blemish-free surface on larger cakes I would always recommend covering with marzipan.

Sugarpaste (rolled fondant)

Sugarpaste is a very soft and smooth ready-to-roll paste, used primarily for covering cakes. A wide range of ready-made, coloured sugarpaste is available, and you can also add paste food colour (see right) to make even more colour options. Keep any sugarpaste that you are not using sealed in a food-grade, polythene bag to prevent it from drying out.

Top Tip

When colouring large amounts of sugarpaste, dip a cocktail stick into the paste colour, add to a small ball of paste and knead to blend the colour. Knead this into the rest of the sugarpaste until fully blended. Repeat the process until the desired colour is achieved.

Royal icing

Throughout the book I have used royal icing to pipe decorations onto cakes and also to stick finished sugar pieces in place. It is also used to create the basketweave effect on English Country Garden (see pages 82 to 89). If you would like to make your own, a basic royal icing recipe is given on page 33. Alternatively, Squires Kitchen's Instant Mix Royal Icing is a great time-saver and is easy to use: just add water according to the pack instructions and mix (see page 33).

Flower paste

Flower paste contains gum tragacanth, which makes it finer and more pliable paste than sugarpaste and also causes it to dry harder. It is designed for flower making but is also used for modelling small pieces. Ready-made flower pastes are available, such as SK Sugar Florist Paste (SFP); a range of colours is available or you can add paste food colours.

Modelling paste

I use equal amounts of sugarpaste and flower paste to make modelling paste: simply blend the two together and seal in a food-grade polythene bag until you are ready to use it. Ready-made modelling paste, such as SK Mexican Modelling Paste (MMP), is also ideal for this purpose so choose whichever you prefer to work with.

Food colourings

Liquid food colours

Liquid food colours are mainly used for colouring isomalt in this book, but they are also useful for colouring buttercream and sponge cakes, and can be used for surface painting.

Paste food colours

Paste food colours can be used with a variety of mediums such as sugarpaste, flower paste, modelling paste and royal icing. Add the colour using a cocktail stick and knead or mix well to blend the colour. For darker shades where more colour is required, you may find it useful to add the corresponding dust colour (see below) as this will prevent the paste from becoming too sticky.

Dust food colours (powders)

There is huge range of dust food colours available which can be brushed onto the surface of sugar work to add depth to the colour. They are particularly effective on sugar flowers and leaves. Dust colours can also be mixed with clear spirit (such as gin or vodka) to make a quick-drying paint.

Metallic and sparkle dust food colours

Metallic and sparkle colours can be used to add a beautiful sparkling or shimmering effect to the surface of sugar work. Like other dusts, they can be mixed with clear spirit and used for surface painting. Always make sure you choose the edible dusts that are designed for food use, rather than non-toxic craft dusts that are intended for decoration purposes only.

Pollen-style dust food colours

Pollen dusts are useful if you are making sugar flowers and they come in a set of popular colours. Alternatively, you can use semolina mixed with dust food colour.

Top Tip

Always have a sheet of kitchen roll to hand to blot any excess colour from the brush.

Bridal Corsages

Edibles

6 round mini cakes with filling (see page 32)

420g (14¾oz) marzipan (SK) (to cover 6 mini cakes)

420g (14¾oz) ivory sugarpaste (to cover 6 mini cakes)

180g (6¼oz) white modelling paste (made from 90g SK Sugar Florist Paste and 90g sugarpaste)

300g (10½oz) royal icing

Silver ball dragées (SK)

Magic Sparkle and Topaz lustre dust food colours (SK)

Equipment

Set of rose petal cutters (FMM)

6 small, round cake cards or circles of greaseproof paper

No. 1 piping nozzle

Ribbon of your choice (to trim cakes)

Basic cake covering and decorating essentials (see page 40)

Preparing the Cakes

1 Prepare the cakes following the instructions for individual mini cakes on page 32. Cover each cake with marzipan then ivory sugarpaste, then trim the base with your choice of ribbon.

2 Make all the corsages separately (2 of each design) a few days before you wish to serve the cakes. Stick the corsages in position with some royal icing and trim the base of the cakes with ribbon.

Corsage 1

1 Roll out 30g of white modelling paste to a thickness of 2-3mm. Cut out 5 rose petals with the second largest cutter, 3 petals with third largest cutter and 3 petals with second smallest cutter.

2 Place the large and medium size petals onto the paint palette to form a cupped shape. Leave for a few minutes to dry slightly.

3 Roll a 1cm ball of modelling paste and wrap the 3 small petals around the ball as shown in the picture (see page 45). Secure the petals in place with edible glue to form the bud.

4 Turn over the large petals and stick them together. Place the 3 medium

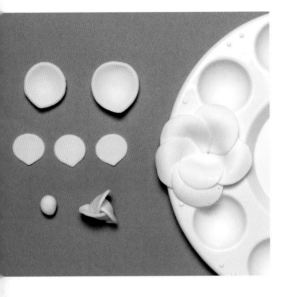

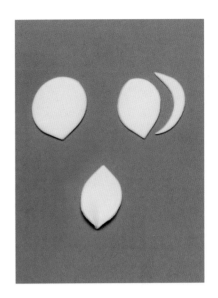

petals upside down inside the large petals and stick them in place with edible glue. Glue the bud in the centre of the flower and allow to dry.

5 When the flower is dry, paint with Topaz iridescent food dust mixed with clear alcohol or dipping solution.

Corsage 2

1 Follow exactly same the method for corsage 1 but make all the petals one size smaller. Instead of making the buds as a centre, roll a small ball of modelling paste.

2 When dry, make up some royal icing to semi-soft peak consistency and place into a piping bag with a no. 1 nozzle. Pipe tiny circles all over the flower. For

the centre, use a cocktail stick to hold it in place and pipe circles over the entire surface. Let it dry then glue it in the centre of the flower.

Corsage 3

1 Roll out some white modelling paste to a 2mm thickness. Cut out 5 rose petals with the second largest cutter. Pinch the edge of petals to make them pointed. Arrange in a circle on a paint palette and let them dry slightly.

2 Make 3 more petals in the same way using the next smallest cutter. Place them in the centre of the flower.

3 Using the same cutter as in step 2, cut out several petal shapes for the leaves. After cutting out the shape, cut one side of

petal again to create a rugby ball shape. Pinch the edges and allow to dry.

4 Brush Topaz food dust mixed with clear alcohol or dipping solution all over the surface of the flowers. Brush some edible glue on the edge of each petal and sprinkle Magic Sparkle dust on top. Brush off the excess sparkle using a soft brush.

5 Stick 3 dragées in the centre of the flower using edible glue.

Top Tip

If you find making individual mini cakes difficult, you can always decorate cupcakes instead.

Damask Design

Edibles

10cm (4") square cake (4 layers)

15cm (6") square cake (2 layers)*

18cm (7") square cake (4 layers)

20cm (8") square cake (2 layers)*

25cm (10") square cake (4 layers)

800g (1lb 12¼oz) royal icing

2.8kg (6lb 2¾oz) filling

820g (1lb 13oz) sugar syrup

3.7kg (8lb 2½oz) marzipan (SK)

2.7kg (5lb 15¼oz) white sugarpaste

1kg (2lb 3¼oz) ivory sugarpaste

Leaf Green paste food colour (SK)

Basic cake covering and decorating essentials (see page 40)

Equipment

10cm, 15cm, 18cm, 20cm, 25cm and 2 x 30cm (4", 6", 7", 8", 10" and 2 x 12") square cake drums

8 plastic cake dowels**

2.5m (8' 2") x 15mm width green satin ribbon

1.5m (4'11") x 15mm width ivory satin ribbon

1.3m x (4' 3") x 30mm width green satin ribbon

Decorations for the cake board

*Bake half the quantity of cake mix to make 2 layers.

**If you are planning to transport the cake, use heavy-duty cake dowels.

Pattern Options

The beauty of this cake is that you can alter the design easily. I have created 3 different effects here, so choose the one that you like best, or make a design of your own! For each of the patterns you will need the following items in addition to those listed on the left:

Plain embossed pattern

1.5m (4' 11") x 20mm width silver ribbon with 2 diamante buckles

Damask design foam craft stamp+

Gilded embossed pattern

Damask design foam craft stamp+

Classic Gold metallic dust food colour (SK)

1.47m (4' 10") x 15mm width ivory satin ribbon

2.8m (9' 2") brocade ribbon

3 gold satin bows

Royal iced pattern

1kg (2lb 3¼oz) royal icing (SK)

Template made from embosser (see page 114)

Cellophane

Masking tape

No. 1.5 piping nozzle

1.5m (4' 11") x 15mm width white lace ribbon

Stick-on jewels (for base board)

+The stamp used on this cake is a foam stamp from a craft shop. A square design works best on this cake: choose one that is no bigger than 8cm (3"). Make sure the stamp you choose is approved for food contact.

Covering the Cakes

1 Stick the 2 x 30cm square cake drums together with royal icing then stick the 25cm cake drum on top. Layer and fill the 25cm square sponge cake then cover with 1.4kg of marzipan.

2 Colour the white sugarpaste pale green using Leaf Green paste food colour and use 1.4kg to cover the cake. As soon as the cake is covered, make the damask patterns on the sides of the cake by pushing the stamp carefully onto the sugarpaste. Cover the edges of the base board with the same green sugarpaste.

3 Prepare the 10cm and 18cm square cakes with marzipan and green sugarpaste, using 500g and 800g respectively. Emboss the pattern onto the cake sides as soon as each cake is covered.

4 For the 15cm and 20cm square cakes, use only 2 layers of cake. Fill and then cover them with marzipan and ivory sugarpaste. You will need approximately 350g and 500g respectively.

5 Dowel all the cakes except the top tier and stack them on top of each other, using royal icing to secure them in place. Take extra care when stacking the cakes so as not to damage the patterns on the sides.

6 Decorate each tier with co-ordinating ribbon, depending on the design you have chosen to make.

Gilded Design

Paint inside the embossed patterns with a mixture of gold metallic food dust and clear spirit.

Royal Iced Design

1 Cut 26-28 squares of cellophane a few centimetres bigger than the embosser design. Make a template of the embosser and place it under a square of cellophane. Grease the cellophane with white vegetable fat (to ensure the run-outs can be released easily) and tape down the corners with masking tape.

2 Pipe the outline of the design in soft-peak royal icing with a no. 1.5 piping nozzle. Secure the template under another piece of greased cellophane and repeat. You will need to make 24 run-outs altogether, plus a few spares to allow for breakages.

3 Once you have piped the outlines, add some cold water to the royal icing to make it run-out consistency (see page 35). Place into a piping bag, snip off the end and flood the designs with the icing. Allow to dry under a lamp or in a warm, dry place. When the icing has hardened, allow to dry fully overnight.

4 Carefully peel the cellophane off the back of each run-out and stick them on the sides of cakes with dots of soft-peak royal icing. Do not press too hard otherwise the run-outs will break.

5 Trim the ivory cakes with ivory ribbon and lace. For extra decoration, stick some press-on jewels to the base board.

Sealed Present Boxes

Edibles

6 square mini cakes with filling (see page 32)

360g (12¾oz) marzipan (SK) (to cover 6 mini cakes)

600g (1lb 5¼oz) white sugarpaste (400g to cover 6 mini cakes + 200g for decoration)

Bluebell, Holly/Ivy, Jet Black and Poinsettia paste food colours (SK)

CMC powder (SK)

Confectioners' glaze (SK)

Equipment

6 small, square cake cards or squares of greaseproof paper

1.8cm (¾") round cutter

Wax seal

Basic cake covering and decorating essentials (see page 40)

Covering the Cakes

1 Colour 200g of sugarpaste pale aqua and 200g darker aqua using Holly/Ivy and Bluebell paste food colours.

2 Cover the 6 mini cakes with marzipan following the instructions on page 32. Cover 3 cakes with the pale aqua sugarpaste and the other 3 with the darker shade.

Decoration

3 Knead a small amount of CMC powder into the remaining 200g of white sugarpaste to make the paste more pliable.

4 Roll out the white sugarpaste very thinly and cut out 270 circles with a 1.8cm diameter round cutter. (You will need 45 circles per cake.) Stick them onto the cakes with small amount of edible glue, starting at the top and working down the sides. Trim the circles to fit if necessary.

5 Add red paste food colour to the remaining sugarpaste. Thinly roll out the red sugarpaste so that it is long enough to go over the top and sides of the cake and cut out a narrow strip. Brush some edible glue on the surface of the cake where you would like to place the strip. Trim one end of the strip neatly and attach it onto

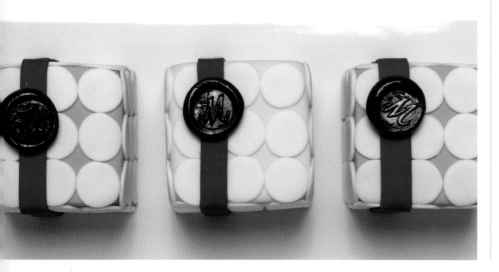

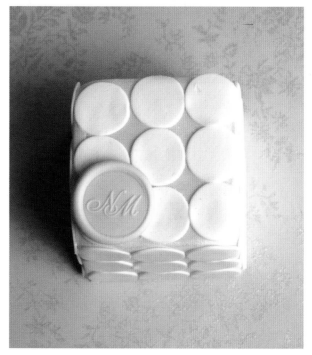

the cake, starting from the bottom on one side. Trim off the excess from the other side with a small palette knife. Repeat for all 6 cakes.

6 Add a tiny amount of black paste food colour to the remaining red sugarpaste to make it a slightly darker colour. Roll a 1cm diameter ball of the paste, flatten the centre with your finger then press it with the wax seal. Attach it to the cake with edible glue and brush with confectioners' glaze to make it shiny. Do the same for the other 5 cakes to finish. Clean the brush with glaze cleaner.

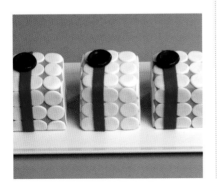

Alternative designs

You can use the same basic method for the cakes but change the wax seal design to make cakes for other special occasions.

Buttons

These make great gifts for a christening or baby shower.

Roll out a small amount of sugarpaste to approximately 3mm thick. Cut out a 2cm circle with a cutter then emboss a slightly smaller circle with another cutter. Mark 4 dots in the centre with a pointed modelling tool or cocktail stick.

Lips

The perfect present for the one you love.

Make 2 small balls from red or pink paste and roll into rugby ball shapes. Make a dent in one of them using your finger to make it look like the top lip shape. Mark fine lines along the edges using a knife.

Sakura Cherry Blossom

Antique Blossom Lace Cake

Edibles

10cm and 20cm (4" and 8") round cakes

250g (8¾oz) sugar syrup

900g (1lb 15¾oz) filling

1.25kg (2lb 12¼oz) soft pink sugarpaste (coloured with a small amount of Cyclamen paste food colour)

1.25kg (2lb 12¼oz) marzipan (SK)

Berberis (ivory) and Cyclamen (SK) paste food colours

200g (7¼oz) white modelling paste (made from 100g SK Sugar Florist Paste and 100g sugarpaste)

100g (3½oz) royal icing, made to soft-peak consistency

Equipment

4 plastic cake dowels

10cm and 20cm (4" and 8") round cake drums

Set of 5-petal blossom cutters (FMM or similar)

Small rose petal cutter (FMM) or a small triangle cutter (Guy Paul & Co.)

Set of round cutters (Guy Paul & Co.)

No. 3 piping nozzle (to make holes)

1.07m (42") 15mm width ivory satin ribbon

Flower templates (see page 114)

Basic cake covering and decorating essentials (see page 40)

Covering the Cakes

1 Prepare the cakes following the instructions for preparing a round cake (see pages 23 to 27). Place the cakes on a sheet of greaseproof paper.

2 Cover the cakes with marzipan then with soft pink sugarpaste. Following the dowelling instructions (see page 31), stack the small cake centrally on the large cake.

3 As there is no cake board underneath the base tier, keep the cake on greaseproof paper until you decorate the cake on a cake stand. Attach satin ribbon around each cake, securing the overlap at the back with double-sided tape.

Lace Pieces

1 Knead the white modelling paste well until the paste becomes smooth and stretchy. Add a small amount of Berberis paste food colour to make ivory.

2 Grease a non-stick board with white vegetable fat then roll out the paste thinly.

3 Cut out several blossom shapes using the different sizes of cutters. You will need approximately 20-25 large, 30-35 medium and 40-45 small blossoms altogether to

cover both cakes. Cut a little V shape from the edge of each petal with the pointed end of a small rose petal cutter or a small triangle cutter.

4 Take 2 different sizes of blossoms and glue the smaller blossoms on top of the larger ones with edible glue, making sure that the petals are lined up. Make 3 holes in the centre with a no. 3 piping nozzle.

5 Again, take 2 sizes of blossoms and glue them together, this time arranging the petals at different angles. Make a hole in the centre with a small, round cutter.

6 Pick up the lace pieces one at a time with a small palette knife, brush some edible glue on the back and place on the surface of the cake randomly until it is completely covered.

7 Prepare the ivory-coloured, soft-peak royal icing in a piping bag and pipe dots on the cake to fill the empty spaces.

Flower

1 Roll out the leftover white modelling paste thinly on a non-stick board.

2 Cut out one of each size flower using the templates.

3 Place each flower onto a foam pad and use a ball tool to frill the edges of the petals. Leave them dry on a palette.

4 When the flowers are semi-dry, stick the small flower onto the large one with a small amount of edible glue.

5 Stick the flower on the cake with a little royal icing icing and pipe a few dots in the centre of the flower.

Falling Blossoms Cake

Edibles

13cm and 18cm (5" and 7") round sponge cakes

240g (8½oz) sugar syrup

800g (1lb 14oz) filling

1.2kg (2lb 10¼oz) marzipan (SK)

1.2kg (2lb 10¼oz) ivory sugarpaste

20g (¾oz) White Sugar Florist Paste (SFP) (SK)

Pastel Pink dust food colour (SK)

100g (3½oz) royal icing: pale pink

Equipment

13cm and 18cm (5" and 7") round cake drums

2 plastic cake dowels

Set of 5-petal blossom cutters (FMM)

Small rose petal cutter (FMM)

Ball tool

1.1m (43½") x 15mm width ivory satin ribbon

Basic cake covering and decorating essentials (see page 40)

Top Tip

Tall cake stands add extra height to cakes with only 1 or 2 tiers.

Covering the Cakes

1 Layer and fill the cakes following the instructions on pages 23 to 27. Place the cakes on a sheet of greaseproof paper.

2 Cover with the cakes with marzipan then with ivory sugarpaste (see page 26).

3 Dowel and stack the cakes (see page 31) and place on a cake stand. Trim the bottom of each tier with 15mm width satin ribbon, securing the overlap with double-sided tape at back of the cake.

Blossom Flowers and Petals

1 Knead the white flower paste well until it becomes smooth and stretchy. Grease a non-stick board with white vegetable fat then roll out the paste thinly.

2 Cut out 3 or 4 flowers with a large blossom cutter. Cut a small V shape from the tip of each petal using a small rose petal cutter.

3 Place the petals onto a foam pad and use a ball tool to press onto the paste and soften the edge slightly. Use the same tool to make a dent in the centre of each petal. Allow to dry on a piece of foam sponge.

4 Repeat steps 1 to 3 to make 5 or 6 small flowers with a small blossom cutter and 5 or 6 petals with a small rose petal cutter. Allow all the flowers and petals to dry on a piece of sponge.

5 Using a dry, flat brush, apply some pale pink dust colour in the centre of each blossom and on the tips of the petals.

6 Prepare the semi-soft peak pale pink royal icing in a piping bag and cut small hole at the tip. Pipe dots in the centre of the flowers.

Decorating the Cake

1 For the top tier, pipe lines using soft-peak, white royal icing to resemble tree branches, making them thicker at the top

and gradually getting thinner towards the bottom. Repeat for the base tier from the top edge to the bottom.

2 Using pale pink, soft-peak royal icing, pipe groups of 5 dots along the sides of the stems.

3 Arrange the prepared sugar flowers on the cake and secure in place with royal icing.

Sakura Cookies

This cookie is called 'sablé diamant' in France. Usually you roll the dough into long rolls that are coated with sugar before slicing, so that the edges of the finished cookies sparkle like a diamond. Two different ways of presenting the cookies are given here, one for a table display and one as a wedding favour or gift.

Recipe

Ingredients

225g (8oz) unsalted butter (at room temperature)

100g (3½oz) icing sugar

70g (2½oz) ground almonds

20ml (¾fl oz) milk

240g (8½oz) plain flour

50g (1¾oz) strong flour

Caster sugar or granulated sugar for coating

Equipment

Mixer

Baking paper

Baking trays

Long, sharp knife

Makes 3 logs (approximately 50 cookies)

1 Cream the butter and icing sugar together. Add the ground almonds and mix through.

2 Add the milk then fold the plain and strong flours together. Mix until combined (do not over-mix).

3 Divide the dough into 3 and roll each piece into a long log. Chill in the fridge for an hour.

Top Tip

If the dough is too sticky, keep it in the fridge until chilled before rolling out into log shapes.

4 Sprinkle plenty of granulated sugar or caster sugar on a sheet of baking paper. Brush the outside of the log with water and roll it in the sugar.

5 Cut 1cm thick circles from the logs with a large, sharp knife. Place them on a baking sheet lined with baking paper, leaving enough space between each one for the dough to spread during cooking.

6 Bake in a preheated oven at 180°C/355°F/gas mark 4 for 10-12 minutes then allow to cool.

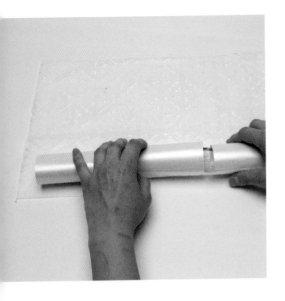

Cherry Blossom Cookie Crackers

Edibles

30-36 Sakura cookies (see opposite)

Equipment

6 A4 sheets of cellophane

Floral wires, ribbon or sticky tapes

9 A4 sheets pale pink writing paper

6 sheets washi (or other thin) paper cut
into 25cm x 35cm rectangles

Double-sided tape

6 cracker snaps

1 long tube with a diameter slightly larger
than the cookies (a kitchen roll tube is
ideal)

Ribbon

Makes 6

1 Make the cookies as described
and wrap in groups of 5 or 6 in sheets
of cellophane. Tie the ends of the
cellophane with floristry wires, ribbon or
sticky tape.

2 Cut 9 A4 sheets of writing paper in
half lengthways to make rectangles
approximately 10cm x 30cm in size.

3 Using a kitchen roll inner tube
or similar as a size guide, make 18
cylinders and secure with double-sided
tape. Put the tube of wrapped cookies
inside 6 cylinders.

4 Place a pre-cut piece of washi paper
onto the work surface. Place a cylinder
with cookies inside in the centre of the
paper and 2 empty cylinders on both
ends. Leave a little space between them.

5 Place a cracker snap inside the
cylinders. Stick a piece of double-sided
tape on the end of the paper and roll it

up around all 3 cylinders together. Seal
with double-sided tape.

6 Tie a piece of ribbon on either side of
the central cylinder.

Iced Sakura Cookies

In addition to the edibles and equipment listed on page 40, you will also need the following:

Edibles

About 50 small cookies (see page 60)

600g (1lb 1½oz) royal icing

Cyclamen liquid food colour (SK)

Pastel Pink dust food colour (SK)

Equipment

Large and small knives

Paper piping bags

Large plastic piping bags

2 bowls

Flat dusting brush: no. 10 (SK)

1 Follow steps 1 to 3 of the recipe to make the cookie dough.

2 Take the dough out of the fridge and flatten one side of the dough with the palm of your hand to make a teardrop shape.

3 Using a large knife, cut it into pieces 1cm thick. Using a small, sharp knife, cut a V shape from the round side of each cookie. Place them on a baking sheet lined with baking paper, leaving enough space between each one for the dough to spread during cooking.

4 Bake in a preheated oven at 180°C/355°F/gas mark 4 for 10-12 minutes then allow to cool.

5 Prepare some soft-peak royal icing with a tiny amount of Cyclamen liquid food colour to make very pale pink. Pipe the outline of a cherry blossom petal on each cookie.

6 Place some of the pink icing into another bowl and add some cold water to make it run-out consistency (when you cut through the icing it should flow together after 10 seconds, see page 35). Place in a large plastic piping bag, snip off the tip and pipe it within the outlines on the cookies. Allow to set.

7 Once the icing has set, brush some Pastel Pink dusting powder on the centre of each cookie. Use the soft peak pink icing to pipe 3 lines from the point.

Temari

Edibles

Sponge cake mix for 20cm (8") round recipe (see page 8)

100g-200g (3½oz-7¼oz) sugar syrup

600g (1lb 5¼oz) buttercream (you will need 40g for each large cake and 20g for each small cake)

400g (14¼oz) jam (you will need 30g for each large cake and 10g for each small cake)

800g (1lb 12¼oz) marzipan (you will need 60g-70g for each large cake and 10g-15g for each small cake)

800g (1lb 12¼oz) white or red sugarpaste, depending on which theme you choose (quantities as per marzipan)

Bag of royal icing

Extra decoration:
Red flower theme

Magic Sparkles and Topaz metallic lustre dust food colours (SK)

Red sugar sprinkles

Poinsettia paste food colour (SK)

Snowflake theme

White Bridal Satin metallic lustre dust food colours (SK)

Silver star sugar sprinkles

Ice White Magic Fairy Sparkle dust food colour (SK)

Equipment

7cm or 4.5cm (2¾" or 1½") half-ball flexible baking pan

Plastic piping bag (optional)

Melon scoop/teaspoon

Pair of food-grade plastic gloves

Small rolling pin

20 small, round cake cards

Extra decoration:
Snowflake theme

No. 1.5 piping nozzle

Cellophane

Snowflake template (see page 114)

Makes 10 large and 10 small temari balls

Basic cake covering and decorating essentials (see page 40)

Making the Spherical Cakes

1 Using the 20cm round Victoria sponge recipe, make the cake mix in the usual way. Place the mixture into a large piping bag and pipe into the half-ball mould. To avoid wastage, pipe the mix from the bottom and work in a circular movement to fill the mould. If you find this difficult, pipe each mould up to ²/₃ full then push the mix towards the edges using a spoon.

2 Bake the cakes at 180°C/355°F/gas mark 4 for 10-20 minutes for the small size, or 20-30 minutes for the large size. Allow to cool in the bakeware.

3 Once cooled, level off the sponges with a large, serrated knife. Using a melon scoop or a small spoon, make a hole in the centre of each cake. Brush syrup over the surface of the cakes.

4 Fill half the cakes with buttercream and the other half with jam, then stick them together in pairs to make ball shapes. Place in the fridge to chill.

5 Put on a pair of food-grade plastic gloves then spread some buttercream over the surface of the cakes. Leave to chill in the fridge again.

If you don't have the flexible baking pans you can use metal half-sphere moulds as an alternative. If you are using a metal mould, brush with melted butter and then dust with flour before piping the mix into the moulds.

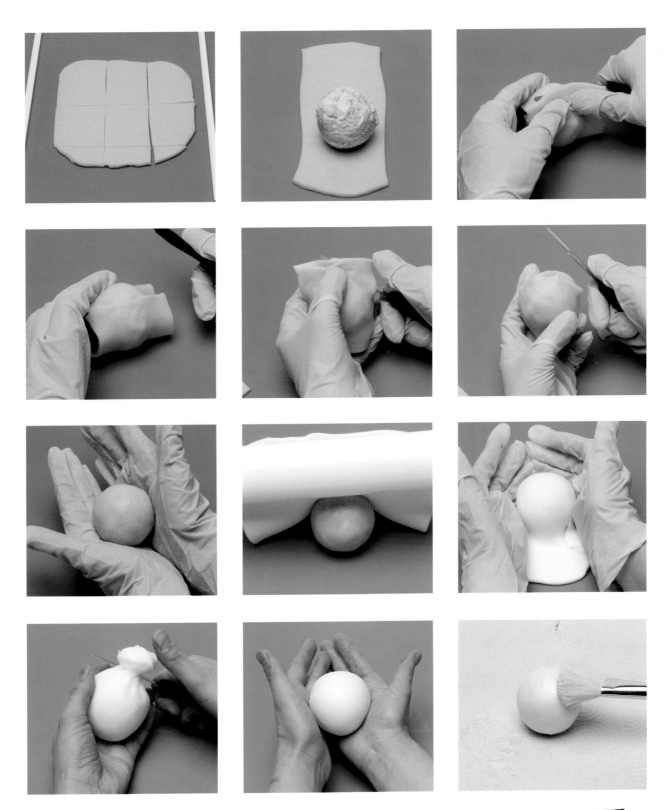

Covering with Marzipan

1 Roll out some marzipan between spacers for an even thickness. Cut it into small pieces then roll further with a small rolling pin until they are large enough to cover the sphere. Place the sponge in the centre, gently wrap the rectangle over the sponge and trim off the top. Squeeze one side then trim away the excess paste using a small palette knife. Repeat on the other side. Make sure the marzipan has an even thickness.

2 Once you have cut off all the excess marzipan, use both hands to gently roll it into a smooth ball. Wearing a pair of food-grade plastic gloves for this helps to keep the covering smooth.

Covering with Sugarpaste

1 Roll out some sugarpaste between spacers, then roll it further to make it a little thinner than usual. Make sure it is large enough to cover the whole surface of the cake (in the same way as for covering a round cake).

2 Lift the sugarpaste over the cake and gently pat it into the ball shape. Lift the whole cake and trim off any excess paste at the bottom. Smooth with both hands (don't wear gloves for this part as this creases the icing).

Top Tip

For small cakes, roll the marzipan and sugarpaste as thinly as possible to keep the flavours balanced.

Decorating the Cakes: Red Flower Theme

For this festive theme I have used 3 easy but attractive methods to decorate the cakes in the display.

Piped loops with red sugar sprinkles

1 Dust the cakes with Topaz shimmer dust while the sugarpaste is still soft.

2 Prepare some red soft-peak royal icing in a piping bag and make a small cut in the tip. Place each cake on a small cake card, securing in place with the red royal icing. Pipe from the top to the bottom in small loops.

3 While the icing is still soft, sprinkle red sugar sprinkles over the cake.

Red sugar sprinkles with sparkle

1 Pour some red sugar sprinkles and Magic Sparkle dust into a small, shallow bowl. Brush clear spirit over the cakes and dab off the excess with kitchen paper. Dip the cake into the sprinkles/sparkle and roll it around until the surface is completely covered.

2 Place each cake on a small cake card, securing in place with red royal icing.

Shimmer dust

1 Dust with Topaz shimmer dust while the sugarpaste is still soft.

2 Place each cake on a small cake card, securing in place with red royal icing.

Decorating the Cakes: Snowflake Theme

Make the piped snowflakes a day in advance to give them time to dry.

1 Prepare the snowflake template and place a sheet of cellophane on top.

2 Prepare some soft-peak royal icing in a piping bag with a no. 1.5 piping nozzle.

3 Pipe the snowflakes onto the cellophane. As soon as they are piped, sprinkle with Magic Fairy Sparkle dust and leave them to dry completely.

4 To decorate the cakes, brush the White Satin Bridal dust all over the surface while the sugarpaste is still soft.

Top Tip

Pipe extra snowflakes to allow for breakages.

5 Attach each cake to a small cake card with a little royal icing then place the cake and card on a titling turntable.

6 Use any sharp tool to mark a cross on the top of the cake, then mark another cross at 45° to divide it into 8.

7 Prepare some stiff-peak royal icing, place it into a piping bag and cut a V in the tip of the bag.

8 Pipe a pattern of 4 leaves on top of the cake and pipe another 4 leaves in between them. Pipe more leaves in the gaps and randomly on the sides of the cake. Allow to dry.

9 Mix some White Satin Bridal dust with clear spirit and brush it onto the piped leaves.

10 Carefully remove the snowflakes from the cellophane and stick them to the cakes with royal icing.

Wedding Bells

Edibles

10cm (4") round cake (4 layers)

13cm (5") round cake (2 layers)*

20cm (8") round cake (4 layers)

25cm (10") square cake (2 layers)*

30cm (12") square cake (4 layers)

3.35kg (7lb 6¼oz) filling

1.07kg (2lb 5¾oz) sugar syrup

4.75kg (10lb 7½oz) marzipan (SK)

4.75kg (10lb 7½oz) white sugarpaste

200g (7¼oz) white modelling paste (made from 100g Sugar Florist Paste and 100g sugarpaste)

Hyacinth paste food colour (SK)

1.4kg (3lb 1¼oz) royal icing (SK)

Any food colour pen (SK)

* Bake half the quantity of cake mix to make 2 layers.

Equipment

Templates (see page 115)

2 x 10cm**, 13cm and 2 x 20cm (4", 5" and 2 x 8") round cake drums

25cm, 2 x 30cm and 35cm (10", 2 x 12" and 14") square cake drums

8-10 plastic cake dowels

No.1.5 piping nozzle

Side design template, drawn onto paper (see page 115)

Sticky tape

Wire cutters

4m (13' 2") x 5mm width white satin ribbon

2m (6' 7") x 15mm width white satin ribbon

Set of small, heart shaped cutters (FMM)

10-12 x 33-gauge and 3 x 18-gauge white floristry wires

White floristry tape

** If you can't find 10cm (4") cake drums, use a cake card and add an extra layer of cake to build up the height.

Basic cake covering and decorating essentials (see page 40)

Covering the Cakes

1 Level and fill the cakes (see page 26) and place each cake onto a corresponding cake drum.

2 Cover each of the 5 tiers as follows:

• 10cm round cake: level and fill 4 layers of cake on 2 cake drums. Cover with 400g marzipan and 400g pale blue sugarpaste.

• 13cm round cake: level and fill 2 layers of cake on 1 cake drum. Cover with 250g marzipan and 250g pale blue sugarpaste.

• 20cm round cake: level and fill 4 layers of cake on 2 cake drums. Cover with 850g marzipan and 850g pale blue sugarpaste.

• 25cm square cake: level and fill 2 layers of cake on 1 cake drum. Cover with 700g marzipan and 700g pale blue sugarpaste.

• 30cm square cake: level and fill 4 layers of cake on 2 cake drums. Cover with 2kg marzipan and 2kg pale blue sugarpaste.

Dowelling the cakes

3 Place the 30cm (12") square cake on the 35cm (14") cake drum then dowel the cakes (see page 31) as follows:

- Dowel the 30cm square cake with 4-6 dowels.
- Dowel the 25cm square cake with 4 dowels.

- Dowel the 20cm round cake with 4 dowels.

- Dowel the 13cm round cake with 4 dowels.

4 Stack the cakes on top of each other, using royal icing to secure each tier in place. Decorate each tier and the base board with satin ribbon.

Top Tip

If you are using fruit cake for any of the tiers, use a heavy duty cake board or one more extra cake board underneath to support the weight of the cake.

Wedding Bells Decoration

Make the cake top decoration a day in advance to allow for drying time.

Heart stems

1 Cut all the 33-gauge floristry wires into 8 equal pieces.

2 Roll out some white modelling paste to a 2mm thickness and cut out 4 different sized heart shapes.

3 Moisten the end of the wires with a little edible glue, insert them into the hearts and pinch the middle to create movement. Allow to dry on a sponge pad or on sheets of kitchen paper.

4 Cut some white floristry tape in half and tape between 6 and 8 hearts together, starting with the smallest one at the top and working down to the largest one.

5 Repeat the same method to make approximately 12 branches altogether.

6 Attach half of the branches to an 18-gauge wire using floristry tape, starting at the top and working down to halfway. Bend the wires into shape to create a natural arrangement. Repeat for the other branches on another 18-gauge wire.

Hanging Bells

7 Cut an 18-gauge wire in half and make a hook in one end.

8 Roll 20g of modelling paste into an egg shape and hollow out the wide end using a small rolling pin. Model it into a bell shape using your hands.

9 Roll out some modelling paste to a thickness of 2mm and cut a narrow strip long enough to go around the base of the bell. Stick it in place with a small amount of edible glue.

10 Moisten the hooked end of the wire with edible glue and insert the straight end

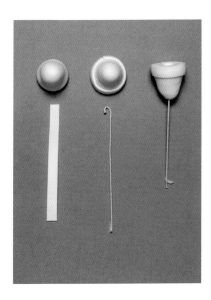

into the bottom of the bell. Pull the wire through until the hook is embedded in the middle of the bell.

11 Repeat steps 7 to 10 to make another bell and allow to dry.

12 Roll 2 x 1cm balls from the leftover white modelling paste and stick one under each bell.

Assembly

13 Tie the 18-gauge wires together with floristry tape at the bottom of each stem. Make a heart shape and fix the ends together. Cut off the excess wire with wire cutters.

Piping Work

Top and Bottom Tiers

1 Measure the height of the top tier and cut a strip of paper to the same height. Wrap the paper around the cake to measure the circumference and cut it 1cm bigger to allow for the join. Check that the paper fits the cake exactly as it will need to be accurate.

2 Fold the paper into 6, leaving 1cm spare at the end. Draw a curve and cut it out with scissors.

3 Open up the paper and wrap it around the cake. Overlap the ends and secure the join with sticky tape.

Top Tip

If you find it difficult to draw the shape freehand, use a metal circle cutter as a guide.

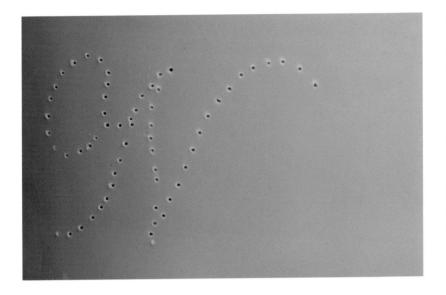

4 For the bottom tier, measure the size of one of the cake sides and cut a piece of paper to fit. Fold the paper into 4, draw a curve and cut it out with scissors.

5 Hold the template against each side of the cake in turn and make tiny dot marks along the template using a scriber tool. Repeat on the top tier with the template then remove the templates.

6 Prepare some stiff-peak royal icing, place into a piping bag and cut a V shape in the tip using fine scissors. Pipe leaves along the templates on both the top and bottom tiers, following the step-by-step picture as a guide.

Second and Fourth Tiers

7 Using a ruler and a scriber, make a mark at the central point on the front, back and both sides of each cake. Place some royal icing into a piping bag with a no. 1.5 nozzle and pipe the flower patterns from the central point to either side, following the step-by-step picture as a guide.

Central Tier

8 Measure the height and circumference of the cake and cut piece of paper to fit, as for the top tier. Again, allow a 1cm overlap for the join.

9 Take the paper template off the cake and draw the monogram onto the centre of the paper with an edible pen. Attach the paper around the cake and mark the pattern using a scriber.

Top Tip

You can use the monogram template on page 115 or make your own in any size by printing the bride and groom's initials in an ornate font from your computer.

10 Prepare some semi soft-peak royal icing in a piping bag with a no. 1.5 piping nozzle. Take the paper off the cake and pipe the pattern from left to right (or vice versa if you are left-handed).

Cake Top Decoration

1 Insert the prepared wedding bells decoration into a flower pick filled with royal icing. Push the pick into the centre of the top tier.

2 Bend the wire at the end of the bells and hang them on the heart. Hide the join at the top of the heart with a bow made from satin ribbon.

Top Tip

If you are travelling a distance to deliver the cake, it is advisable to assemble the cake top decoration at the venue so that it doesn't get damaged in transit.

Material Girls

White Ring Boxes with Coloured Jewels

Edibles

16 isomalt jewels in different colours (see page 81)

10cm (4") round cake

16 x 5cm (2") round mini cakes

200g (7¼oz) syrup

400g (14¼oz) filling

400g (14¼oz) marzipan (SK)

1.4kg (3lb 1½oz) white sugarpaste

20g (¾oz) White Sugar Florist Paste (SFP) (SK)

Jet Black paste food colour (SK)

200g (7¼oz) royal icing

Silver lustre dust food colour (SK)

Equipment

10cm (4") round cake drum

16 x 5cm (2") small round cake cards or circles of greaseproof paper

Narrow white satin ribbon (for 16 mini cakes)

33cm (13") 15mm width white satin ribbon (for top tier)

Real ring or crystal for the top-tier decoration

Basic cake covering and decorating essentials (see page 40)

Making the Rings

Make the rings a day in advance to allow them to dry hard.

1 Colour 20g of flower paste pale grey using a small amount of Jet Black paste food colour.

2 Roll the paste into a very thin thread shape. Cut it into 16 strips. Curve each one into a C shape and trim to size. Allow to dry.

Making the Ring Boxes

3 Prepare and cover the 16 small, round cakes with white sugarpaste following the instructions on page 32. (I didn't use marzipan as I wanted to make the cakes slightly smaller than usual.)

4 Prepare some soft-peak white royal icing, place into a piping bag and cut off the tip to make a tiny hole. Pipe small dots around the top edge of the cakes.

5 Make 2 small cuts in the top of the 16 small cakes using the tip of a sharp knife. Push the prepared rings into the holes and paint with a mixture of silver dust colour and clear spirit.

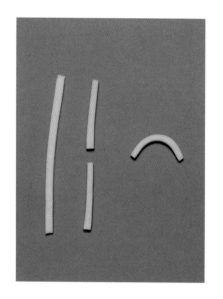

Pastel Ring Boxes with Diamonds

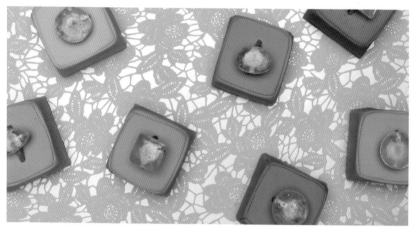

6 Attach the ready-made jewels on top of the rings using a small amount of grey coloured royal icing.

7 To finish, trim the cakes with narrow ribbon and secure at the back with a dot of royal icing or edible glue.

Top Tier

8 Level and fill the 10cm cake then cover the cake with marzipan and white sugarpaste in the usual way (see pages 23 to 27). Place a large crystal on the top tier for decoration.

9 Trim the base of the cake with ribbon, overlap the ends at the back of the cake and secure to itself with double-sided tape.

Top Tip

Instead of the large crystal you could use a real engagement ring as a surprise.

Edibles

16 clear isomalt jewels (see opposite)

16 x 5cm (2") square sponge cakes

1kg (2lb 3¼oz) white sugarpaste

200g (7¼oz) syrup

400g (14¼oz) buttercream

Paste food colours of your choice (SK) (I used Cyclamen for pink, Bluebell for blue, Leaf Green for pale green, Bluegrass for aqua green, Daffodil for yellow, Marigold for orange and Berberis for ivory)

20g (¾oz) White Sugar Florist Paste (SFP) (SK)

Jet Black paste food colour (SK)

100g (3½oz) royal icing

Silver lustre dust food colour (SK)

Equipment

16 x 5cm (2") small square cake cards or squares of greaseproof paper

Stitching tool (PME)

Making the Rings

1 Make the rings from flower paste as described on page 78.

Making the Ring Boxes

2 Prepare and cover the 16 square cakes with coloured sugarpaste following the instructions on page 32. While the paste is still soft, use a stitching tool to mark a dotted line around the top and down the sides of each cake to resemble a box.

3 Make 2 small cuts in the top of the cakes using the tip of a sharp knife. Push the prepared rings into the holes and paint with a mixture of silver dust colour and clear spirit.

4 Attach the ready-made jewels on top of the rings using a small amount of grey coloured royal icing.

Basic cake covering and decorating essentials (see page 40)

Using Isomalt

Edibles

500g (1lb 1½oz) bag of isomalt (SK)

Equipment

Clean copper pan or steel saucepan
Heat-resistant spatula
Sugar thermometer
Silicone paper
Airtight container

1 Place 500g of isomalt into a clean, dry copper or steel saucepan. Stir continuously over a low heat until the isomalt has melted then continue to heat the solution until it reaches 180°C.

2 Remove the pan from the heat and immerse the base in cold water to halt the cooking process and cool the solution.

3 Pour the solution over a sheet of silicone paper and allow to set. When the isomalt has cooled, break into small pieces and store in an airtight container.

4 To use the isomalt, place as many pieces as required into a clean, dry saucepan and heat gently until it has melted. Alternatively, you can use a heat-resistant bowl and heat up the isomalt in the microwave. Once melted, use as required for your chosen project.

Top Tip

The isomalt pieces can be kept in an airtight container for several months so you only need to melt enough for each project.

Making Jewels with Isomalt

Edibles

250g (8¾oz) isomalt pieces (see left)
Liquid food colours of your choice (SK)

Equipment

Great Impressions jewel mould (SK)
Food-grade gloves (plastic or cotton)
Scissors
Saucepan
Spatula
Spoons
Airtight containers

Makes around 50-60 large jewels

1 Heat the isomalt pieces in a pan. Add the liquid colour at this stage if required and stir.

Top Tip

To save using many different liquid colours, remember that you can mix colours to make a wide range, e.g. mix red and blue to make purple.

2 When the mix has melted, use a spoon to pour the isomalt carefully into the jewel mould. Wear the gloves when you do this to protect your hands from the heat. The isomalt sets almost instantly so you will need to work quickly.

3 Once set, turn the jewels out of the mould and keep them in an airtight container until you are ready to use them.

Material Girls

English Country Garden

Cake

Edibles

10cm, 15cm and 20cm (4", 6" and 8")
round and 25cm (10") square cakes
3.25kg (7lb 2¾oz) marzipan (SK)
3.25kg (7lb 2¾oz) ivory sugarpaste
750g (1lb 10½oz) sugar syrup
2.5kg (5lb 8¼oz) filling
12 medium yellow roses (see pages 85 to 86)
15-20 stems of mimosa (see page 87)
30 small daisies (see page 88)
Stripy sugar bow (see page 89)
Berberis (ivory) paste food colour (SK)
2kg (4lb 6¼oz) royal icing

Equipment

12 plastic cake dowels
10cm, 15cm and 20cm (4", 6" and 8")
round; 25cm and 30cm (10" and 12")
square cake drums
Large plastic piping bags
No. 47 basketweave piping nozzle (Wilton)
1.3m (4' 3") x 15mm width ivory satin ribbon
15-20 small flower picks
Wire cutters
Wooden skewers

Basic cake covering and decorating
essentials (see page 40)

Covering and Assembling the Cakes

1 Prepare the 4 cakes following the instructions on page 26.

2 Cover the cakes with marzipan then with a thin coat of ivory sugarpaste (see pages 26 to 27).

Top Tip

The sugarpaste coating should be thinner than normal on this cake, so roll out further after you have removed the spacers. If preferred, you can ice the cake with a base coat of royal icing instead of sugarpaste.

3 Place the bottom tier on the base board and secure ribbon around the edge of the board. Dowel and stack the 4 tiers following the instructions on page 31.

4 Colour the royal icing cream by adding a little Berberis (ivory) paste colour. Place in a piping bag with a basketweave nozzle and pipe woven patterns onto the sides of the cakes, following the step-by-step picture as a guide. Start from the top edge

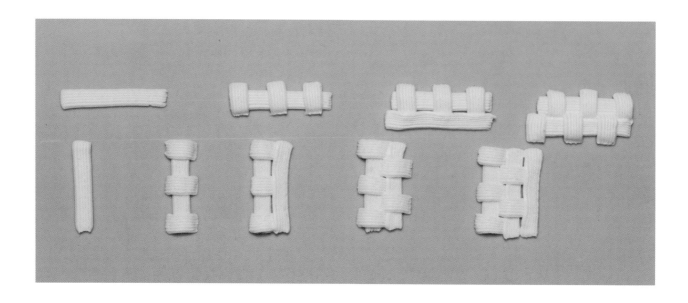

of the top tier and work down. For the 3 round cakes, start with the horizontal lines and pipe the short, vertical lines over the top, starting at the back and working round to the front; for the square cake, pipe the front first, then both sides, and finally the back. Leave to dry. Keep the icing bag for the next step.

Top Tip

The basketweave pattern can be piped horizontal then vertical, or vice versa to create slightly different effects (as shown in the picture above).

Decoration

5 Position the roses around the third tier, making sure that you are happy with the arrangement before sticking them on. Once you have decided, secure them in place with some stiff-peak, ivory coloured icing (left over from earlier).

6 Fill the gaps between the roses using the mimosa stems. To do this, insert a small flower pick into the cake first and pipe some royal icing into the hole. Insert the mimosa stem into the pick, cutting the wire if necessary. If there are any gaps or untidy areas, cover them with individual mimosa buds.

7 Scatter daisies around the arrangement and secure them in place with royal icing.

8 To finish, secure the stripy bow to the second tier with royal icing.

Roses

Edibles

400g (14¼oz) White Sugar Florist Paste (SFP) (SK)

Sunflower paste food colour (SK)

Rose dust food colour (SK)

White vegetable fat

Edible glue (SK)

Equipment

Wooden skewers

Rose petal cutter set (FMM)

Plastic food bags

Polystyrene petal formers/tin foil

Makes 12 medium roses

Basic cake decorating essentials (see page 40)

Centre

Prepare the rose centres the day before making the petals to give them time to dry.

1 Knead approximately half of the white flower paste until it is smooth and stretchy. Add a small amount of Sunflower paste food colour to make a pale yellow paste.

2 Form a small piece (approximately 8g) of the pale yellow paste into a cone shape. Insert a cocktail stick or wooden skewer into the base of the cone and set this aside to dry on a polystyrene dummy. Repeat to make 12 centres altogether.

Top Tip

Keep the flower paste in a plastic food bag when not in use to prevent it from drying out.

Petals

3 Colour some of the remaining flower paste pale yellow, as before. Grease a non-stick board with white vegetable fat then roll out some of the paste thinly.

4 To make the first and second layers of petals, use the third largest cutter to cut out 4 petals. Place a sheet of cling film over the petals when you are not working on them to prevent the paste from drying out.

5 Place a petal onto a foam pad and use a ball tool to soften the edges. To do this, place the tool half on the paste and half on the pad, press down and move the tool around the edge of the petal.

6 Apply edible glue halfway up the length of the petal. Wrap 1 side around the cone then wrap the other over the top.

7 For the second layer of petals, soften the remaining 3 petals on the foam pad then brush edible glue halfway up the

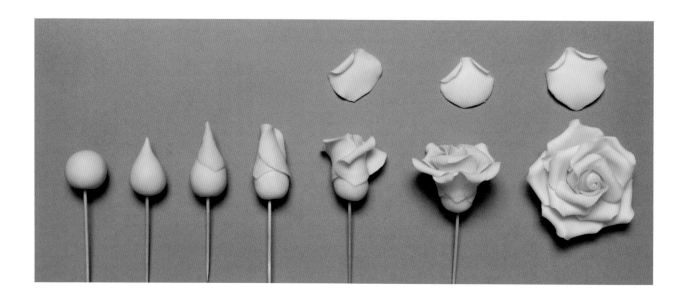

left-hand side of each petal. Stick the first petal to the bud at the same level, leaving the right-hand side unstuck. Stick on the next petal so that it overlaps the first, as shown, leaving the right-hand side unstuck. The left-hand side of this petal should be underneath the first petal. Repeat with the last of these petals, overlapping it in the same way as before.

8 For the third layer of petals, add some more white flower paste to the rest of the yellow paste to make a paler colour. Using the petal cutter the next size up, make 4 more petals and repeat steps 4 to 7. This time, curl one side of petal edges using a cocktail stick before sticking them on. Allow dry on a polystyrene former.

9 To make the fourth layer of petals, add some more white flower paste to the rest of the paste. Using the same size cutter as for the third layer, make 5 petals. Repeat steps 5 to 7 and this time curl both sides of the petal edges with a cocktail stick

before sticking them on. Allow to dry on the polystyrene former, or use a small piece of tin foil if preferred.

10 For the fifth and final layer, add some more white flower paste to the rest of the paste. Using the next size cutter (1 size larger), make 5 petals in the same way as before. Remove the cocktail stick from the base and allow the flower to firm on a paint palette to give it a more natural shape.

11 Repeat this method to make 12 roses altogether. Allow to dry fully before dusting them.

Dusting

12 Place some pink dusting powder on a sheet of kitchen paper. Using a large, soft, flat paintbrush, gently apply a very pale colour to the edge of each petal. Gradually add more colour to deepen the colour until you have a natural finish.

Top Tip

If you find the powder colour too strong, you can always add some icing sugar, white dust colour or cornflour to lighten the tone.

Steaming

13 Insert the skewer back in to the centre of the roses so that you have something to hold, then pass the flowers through steam to set the dust colour and give them slightly shiny, natural look. This also stops the dust colour falling onto the iced cake. I usually use steam from the kettle, leaving the lid slightly open so that the kettle continuously boils. (Some people use confectioners' glaze to finish the flowers but I personally prefer steaming as it is both easy and effective.) Let the flowers dry on the polystyrene dummy.

Mimosa

Edibles

200g (7¼oz) White Sugar Florist Paste (SFP) (SK)

Sunflower and Leaf Green paste food colours (SK)

Sunflower dust food colour (SK)

Semolina

Rose water (or water), boiled and cooled

Equipment

60 x 33-gauge green floristry wires

Pale green floristry tape

Wire cutters

Makes 15-20 mimosa stems

Basic cake decorating essentials (see page 40)

Top Tips

To save time you can cut up to 5 wires at once.

If you are using 10mm width floristry tape, cut it to 5mm wide so that it is easier to handle.

Buds

1 Cut each 33-gauge floristry wire into 8 pieces (it doesn't matter if they are not all the same length). Bend a tiny hook into one end of each piece of wire.

2 Add a tiny amount of Leaf Green paste food colour to 20g (¾oz) of white flower paste then colour the rest of the paste pale yellow by adding a little Sunflower paste food colour.

3 Roll tiny balls (3mm-5mm) from the green paste and cover with a sheet of cling film to prevent the paste from drying out.

4 Moisten the hooked end of a wire with edible glue. Insert the other end of the wire into a ball of paste and thread the ball up the wire to cover the hook. Reshape the ball if necessary. Allow to dry on polystyrene. Repeat with the remaining balls of green paste.

5 Repeat the process again with yellow paste, this time making the balls slightly larger (5mm-10mm).

Assembly

6 Starting with smallest green buds, tape 3 or 4 buds into one stem. Add 4 or 5 small yellow buds down the stem then finish off with a few larger size buds. You should be able to make up to 60 small stems altogether.

7 Tape together 3 small stems to make a large stem. You will need 15-20 of these for the cake.

Pollen Dust

8 Add a small amount of the yellow dust colour to the semolina flour.

9 Brush the rose water onto the mimosa buds, take the excess water off with kitchen paper and dip them into the coloured pollen dust. Shake off any excess pollen and let them dry on a polystyrene dummy.

Small Daisies

Edibles

100g (3½oz) White Sugar Florist Paste
(SFP) (SK)
Sunflower dust food colour (SK)
Sunflower paste food colour (SK)
Semolina

Equipment

Daisy cutter (FMM)
Stay-fresh mat (or cling fillm)

Makes 30 small daisies

Basic cake decorating essentials (see
page 40)

1 Knead the white flower paste well until
the paste becomes smooth and stretchy.

2 Grease a non-stick board with white
vegetable fat then roll out the paste thinly.
Cut out a few flower shapes with a daisy
cutter. Place a stay-fresh mat on top to
prevent the paste from drying out.

3 Place a flower onto a foam pad and
use a Dresden tool to soften the edge of
each petal slightly. Repeat for all the flower
shapes.

4 Stick 2 flowers together with a small
amount of edible glue, positioning the
petals of the top flower between the ones
beneath. Allow to dry on a piece of foam

sponge or a paint palette to form a slightly
cupped shape.

5 Repeat the same method to make 60
flower shapes for 30 daisies altogether.

6 Add some yellow paste food colour
to the remaining flower paste. Make 1cm
diameter balls for the centre of the daisies.

7 Colour the semolina with yellow dust
colour to make the pollen. Moisten the
flower centres with edible glue and drop
them into the semolina pollen to cover
them.

8 Secure a yellow centre to each daisy
with edible glue.

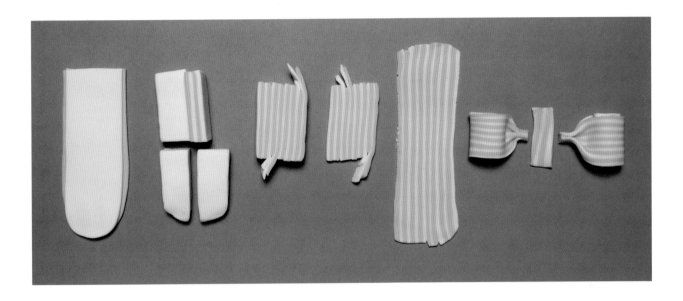

Stripy Sugar Ribbon

Edibles

100g (3½oz) White Sugar Florist Paste
(SFP) (SK)

Sunflower paste food colour (SK)

Basic cake decorating essentials (see
page 40)

1 Add a small amount of yellow paste food colour to half of the white flower paste so that you have equal amounts of yellow and white paste.

2 Make a long sausage shape from both colours and roll out separately into long rectangles approximately 5cm wide and 2mm thick.

3 Place one on top of the other and trim the short edge straight. If the pastes don't stick together, use a little edible glue.

4 Cut the paste in half widthways using a large, sharp knife and place one half on top of the other so that the cut edges line up. This will create a striped pattern at the end. Repeat the same process twice to create 8 yellow and 8 white stripes.

5 Slice the end off the block of paste with a large knife and roll it into a long, narrow strip. Trim off any messy edges.

6 Shape the strips into the parts of the bow, i.e. 2 loops, 2 tails and the knot. Place a roll of kitchen paper inside both loops to hold the shape until the paste is dry.

Fancy Hats

Edibles

18cm (7") round sponge cake

15cm (6") dome shaped sponge cake*

5 x 5cm (2") dome shaped mini cakes*

5 x 5cm (2") round mini cakes**

400g (14¼oz) sugar syrup

1kg (2lb 3¼oz) filling

700g (1lb 8¾oz) marzipan for the large hat, 350g (12¼oz) for the small hats (SK)

800g (1lb 12¼oz) ivory sugarpaste for the large hat, 140g (5oz) for the 2 small hats

210g (7½oz) black sugarpaste for the 3 small hats

CMC powder (SK)

500g (1lb 1½oz) black modelling paste (made from 250g Sugar Florist Paste and 250g sugarpaste)

500g (1lb 1½oz) ivory modelling paste (made from 250g Sugar Florist Paste and 250g sugarpaste)

20g (¾oz) royal icing

Small sliver dragees (SK)

Piping gel (SK) (optional)

Rose paste food colour (SK)

*Use the 13cm (5") round cake recipe to make the large dome and 5 dome mini cakes.

**Use the 13cm (5") round cake recipe and bake in a 15cm (6") square tin to make the 5 round mini cakes.

Equipment

Large circle cutters

Rose petal cutters (FMM)

5-petal flower cutters (FMM)

5 small, round cake cards

13cm and 15cm (5" and 6") round cake drums

2 square cake boards (to use as a thickness guide, optional)

Feather decoration

Flower pick

Assortment of ribbons for each cake

Basic cake covering and decorating essentials (see page 40)

Large Hat Cake

You will need one 15cm round and one 15cm dome shaped cake for the large hat.

1 Trim the crust off the 18cm round sponge cakes and level in the usual way (see pages 23 to 27). You should have 4 slices of cake that are exactly the same thickness and diameter.

2 Level off the 15cm dome shaped sponge cake so that you have a half-sphere shape. Slice it half horizontally.

3 Place the 15cm cake drum on a piece of greaseproof paper then layer and fill the cakes with sugar syrup and your chosen filling with the dome cake on top, following the method on page 26.

4 Cover the cake with marzipan (see page 26).

5 Roll out some black sugarpaste on a non-stick board and cut out a long, shallow curved shape with a flat base. Stick the paste to one side of the cake (see page 93).

6 Roll out 800g of ivory sugarpaste, making sure it is large enough to cover the cake. Lift it carefully and place it on top. Smooth the covering down and around the cake with the palm of your

hand, pressing gently around the sides to remove any air bubbles. Trim away the excess sugarpaste from around the base of the cake using a small palette knife then rub the surface gently with cake smoothers to remove all the air bubbles. Cut along the line of black paste underneath then trim around the base once again to create a neat edge.

Hat Brim

7 Decorate a 13cm round cake drum with your choice of coloured ribbon and attach the cake on top with royal icing. This way you can lift the hat easily and place the cake directly on a cake stand so that it looks more realistic. (If you would like to present it on the larger cake board, please follow the usual method, see pages 28 to 29).

8 Add ½ a teaspoon of CMC powder to the leftover ivory paste and knead well. Seal the paste in a plastic food bag and

allow the paste to rest for a while so that the gum can strengthen the paste.

9 Roll out the strengthened modelling paste and cut out a 23cm diameter circle. Cut out a 14cm circle from the centre to make a doughnut shape. Brush a tiny amount of edible glue along the bottom edge of the hat. Cut through one side of the circle of paste, gently lift it and attach it around the hat with the join opposite the black paste underneath.

10 Cut the brim to the correct length at the back of the cake and blend the join by gently rubbing it with your fingers. Support the lifted side with kitchen paper until dry.

Ribbon

11 Roll out 150g of the ivory modelling paste to a thickness of 1.5cm and cut out a 4cm x 30cm rectangle.

Top Tip

You can use spare cake drums as spacers to give you the correct thickness.

12 Roll out 100g of black modelling paste into a 4cm x 30cm rectangle using marzipan spacers as a guide for the thickness. Repeat to make a second black rectangle.

13 Place a black rectangle on the non-stick board and stick the ivory rectangle on top with tiny amount of edible glue. Stick the other black rectangle on top of the ivory paste. Trim the long edge neatly then cut into slices approximately 1cm thick. Cover the remaining paste with cling film to prevent it from drying out.

14 Gently roll one of the slices of paste into a long strip using a small rolling pin.

Hat 1

Trim the edges neatly then attach the paste around the hat to hide the join between the hat and the brim (you might have to use 2 strips to go all the way around the cake). Attach the ribbon where the bow will be and cut off the join at the back of the hat.

15 Roll out the other strips as before then shape them into the bow loops and knot (see the step-by-step pictures for English Country Garden on page 89). Place some rolled kitchen paper inside the loops to hold the shape until dry, then attach the bow to the hat using edible glue.

(see the step-by-step pictures for English Country Garden on page 89)

Top Tip

Every time you slice the black and white paste, make sure the knife is clean so that the colour is not transferred from one to the other.

Small Hat Cakes

1 Prepare 5 small cakes following the instructions on page 32. Place a dome shaped sponge on top of each one, using buttercream to stick them together.

2 Spread buttercream over the surface of the cake then place on a small cake card or piece of greaseproof paper. Repeat for all 5 cakes and leave to firm in the fridge.

3 Cover the cakes with marzipan and sugarpaste: use black sugarpaste for 3 of the cakes and ivory for the remaining 2.

4 Decorate each cake with your choice of satin ribbon around the base and secure with a little edible glue or royal icing.

Hat 1

1 Roll out some black modelling paste to a thickness of 2mm. Cut out a 5cm circle

following the instructions on page 32

and place it onto a black covered cake at a slight angle.

2 Roll out some more black modelling paste and cut out an 8cm circle. Cut out a 4cm circle from the centre then cut through the paste to open up the circle.

3 Brush some edible glue around the edge of the 5cm circle on top of the cake. Gently lift the ring of paste and attach it around the edge of the circle. Position the join at the lowest part and overlap the ends.

4 Roll out some ivory modelling paste and cut out 8 rose petals with the cutters. Frill the edges of the petals with a cocktail stick and let them dry slightly on a paint palette.

5 When the petals are semi-dry, join them together with edible glue. Roll a small

Hat 2

Hat 3

Hat 4

ball of black paste, brush the centre with edible glue and dip it into the small silver dragées. Stick this to the centre of the flower.

6 Stick the flower onto the cake to hide the join in the brim.

Hat 2

1 Roll out some ivory modelling paste to a thickness of approximately 2mm. Cut out a 7.5cm circle then cut out a 5cm circle $\frac{1}{3}$ from the bottom with a cutter. Cut through the paste to open up the circle.

2 Place the 5cm circle on a black covered cake at a slight angle.

3 Brush some edible glue around the edge of the 5cm circle, gently lift the brim and attach it around the circle. Overlap the 2 ends at the lowest point of the circle (this will be covered by the flower).

4 Roll out some ivory modelling paste to a 2mm thickness and cut out 5 petals with the third largest cutter and 5 petals with the second smallest cutter. Arrange the petals on a paint palette to form the flower shape and leave to firm.

5 Place the large petals upside down and stick them together. Place the 5 small petals inside the large petals and stick them in place with edible glue.

6 Roll a small ball of ivory paste and make a dip in the centre. Stick it inside the flower with edible glue. For added decoration, pipe some piping gel into the centre and drop in a few silver dragées.

Hat 3

1 Roll out some black modelling paste to a thickness of 2mm. Cut out a 7.5cm circle and place it onto a black covered cake at a slight angle.

2 Use the same paste to cut out a strip measuring 2.5cm x 20cm. Cut the ends at an angle so one side measures 18cm and glue it around the circle with the shorter side at the bottom.

3 Roll out the black modelling paste again to a 2mm thickness and cut out a long strip 2cm wide. Cut 2 loops and a knot from the strip and form into a bow, following the step-by-step picture as before. Stick the bow to the centre of the brim to hide the join.

4 Colour some soft-peak royal icing pale pink, place into a piping bag, snip off the end and pipe dots onto the hat.

Hat 4

1 Roll out some black modelling paste to a 2mm thickness. Cut out an 8cm circle and place it onto an ivory covered cake at a slight angle.

Hat 5

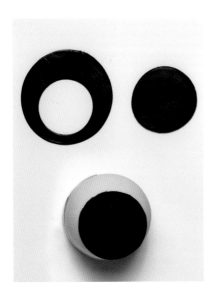

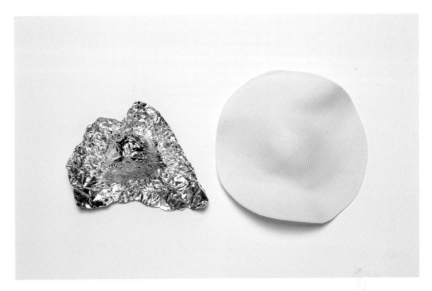

2 Roll out some black modelling paste and cut out a 14cm circle. Cut out a 6cm circle from the centre then cut through the paste to open it up.

3 Brush some edible glue around the edge of the 8cm circle. Gently lift the strip of paste and attach it around the circle. Overlap the ends at the lowest point of the circle.

4 To make the stripy ribbon, roll out some ivory modelling paste to a 5mm thickness and cut a 2.5cm x 18cm rectangle. Repeat with black modelling paste then stick the 2 pastes together with a small amount of edible glue. Cut it into 3 and stick the 3 blocks together with edible glue. The side of the block should now be stripy.

5 Slice a 5mm piece off and roll out gently with a small rolling pin. Trim the edge neatly and wrap it around the hat. Make a bow as previously described and stick this to the front of the hat.

Hat 5

1 Roll out some ivory modelling paste to a 2mm thickness and cut out a 14cm circle. Form the hat shape using tin foil and kitchen paper and use this as a former for the circle of paste. Allow to dry.

2 Roll out some more ivory modelling paste thinly and cut out few small flowers in different sizes. Place the flowers onto a foam pad and frill the edges of each one using a ball tool. Allow to dry.

3 Stick the hat on an ivory covered cake and glue the flowers randomly onto it using edible glue or royal icing. Pipe small dots in the centre of each flower with soft-peak white royal icing.

4 Push a flower pick filled with paste into the top of the hat and insert a feather decoration into the pick.

Top Tip

This design looks equally stylish in bright colours such as pink, yellow and green.

Paper Peonies

Cake

Edibles

10cm-33cm (4"-13") round cakes*

7kg (15lb 7oz) filling

10kg (22lb) marzipan (SK)

10kg (22lb) white sugarpaste

130-150 white rice paper peonies (see pages 100 to 101)

2kg (4lb 6½oz) royal icing

*I used slightly shallower sponge cakes than the usual height because of the large number of tiers. To do this, use the recipe one size smaller and bake it in a tin at the size you require, instead of dividing the mixture into 2 tins. After baking, slice it into 3 layers (rather than 4) using the second notch of the cake leveller. Each tier should be around 8cm (3") high including the cake board.

Alternatively, bake the cakes as normal in the required sizes from 10cm to 25cm (4" to 10") as a 7-tier wedding cake: this will be almost the same height as the 10-tier version.

Equipment

22-24 heavy duty plastic cake dowels

10cm-33cm (4"-13") round cake drums and 46cm (18") cake drum or heavy duty cake drum

Plastic piping bag

1.5m (4' 11") x 15mm width white satin ribbon

Double-sided tape

Makes a 10-tier wedding cake

> **Basic cake covering and decorating essentials (see page 40)**

Making the Cakes

1 Bake all 10 cakes as described then cut and fill with jam and buttercream. Cover with marzipan and white sugarpaste in the usual way (see pages 26 to 27).

2 Dowel all of the cakes except the top tier with plastic dowels (see page 31). You will need to use 6-9 dowels in the lower 5 tiers to support the weight of the cake.

> ### Top Tip
>
> If you don't need all 10 cakes for your guests, you can replace the top tiers with polystyrene dummy cakes for top tiers. You can even replace the top 9 tiers with dummy cakes and only use real cake for the base tier to get the wow factor.

3 Using the 46cm cake drum as a base, trim the edge with 15mm ribbon. Assemble all 10 tiers by carefully placing them on top of each other.

Decoration

4 Place some white royal icing into a large plastic piping bag and use this to

attach the rice paper peonies one-by-one to the cake. Start from the central point at the base of the cake, then place a flower on both sides and repeat until the flowers meet at the back of the cake.

5 Work your way up the tiers until they are completely covered with peonies. Place a large, satin bow on top to finish.

Top Tip

If you are transporting this cake to a wedding it is definitely easier if you assemble it at the venue.

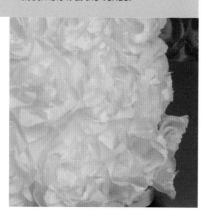

Rice Paper Peonies

Edibles

Large packs of rice paper (the number of sheets will depend on the size – you will need enough to make 130-150 peonies, 8 flower shapes for each peony)

Equipment

Peony templates A-D, drawn onto thin card (see page 116)

Basic cake decorating essentials (see page 40)

1 Draw the peony templates A, B, C and D onto thin card and cut to shape.

2 Cut a large sheet of rice paper into smaller pieces, roughly the same size as each flower template.

3 You need 2 flower shapes in each size to make 1 peony so cut out the flowers in pairs. Hold 2 pieces of rice paper together with the template on top and cut out the flower shape. Remove the template and make a small, rounded V shaped cut between the petals. Gently round off the edges then cut a wavy edge around each petal.

Top Tip

When you are cutting out the flowers, don't worry about cutting the exact shape. The finished peonies will look more natural if the petals are slightly irregular.

Paper Peonies

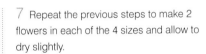

4 Using a clean pastry brush and cooled, boiled water, lightly moisten 1 petal to make it slightly sticky.

5 Place the flower on a piece of soft sponge and push into the middle of the petal with your thumb or the end of a small rolling pin to cup the petals. Gently lift your thumb/the rolling pin off the paper. If the petal does not curl enough, repeat again. (You should find that the petals curl a little more when they have dried out.)

Top Tip

Do not use too much water otherwise the rice paper will disintegrate when you press onto it.

6 Repeat the same method to shape all the other petals on both flowers and let them dry on the sponge.

7 Repeat the previous steps to make 2 flowers in each of the 4 sizes and allow to dry slightly.

8 Moisten the centre of a large flower (D) and place the second flower on top at a slightly different angle. Moisten the centre again and add the 2 size C flowers, then the B flowers, and finally put the smallest flowers (A) inside.

9 Form the shape of the peony using your hands and let it dry on the sponge completely.

Top Tip

The rice paper flowers can be prepared well in advance and they are very easy to transport. If you would like to add colour, brush a little dust food colour onto the petals before sticking the layers together.

Cats and Birds

Edibles

10cm (4") round cake

20cm (8") round cake

1 large size spherical cake* (see Temari on page 64)

10 x 5cm (2") round mini cakes, covered with marzipan (70g per cake) and pink sugarpaste (70g per cake) (see page 32)

1.3kg (2lb 13¾oz) marzipan (SK)

1.3kg (2lb 13¾oz) white sugarpaste

200g (7¼oz) black modelling paste (made from 100g Sugar Florist Paste and 100g sugarpaste)

Cyclamen and Jet Black paste food colours (SK)

600g (1lb 5¼oz) royal icing (SK)

Equipment

Templates, drawn onto thin card (see page 117)

4 plastic cake dowels

4.4m (14' 5") pale pink satin ribbon

10cm, 20cm and 25cm (4", 8" and 10") round cake drums

10 small, round cake cards or circles of greaseproof paper

*If you are making the birdcage for display only, you can use an 8cm (3") diameter polystyrene ball instead of a real cake. These are available from craft shops.

Basic cake covering and decorating essentials (see page 40)

Covering the Cakes

1 Level and fill the 10cm and 20cm round cakes and cover with marzipan in the usual way (see pages 23 to 27). You will need approximately 200g of marzipan for the smaller cake and 700g for the larger one. Colour the sugarpaste pale pink using Cyclamen paste food colour and cover both cakes.

2 Dowel the large cake (see page 31) and place it on top of the 25cm cake drum, securing it in place with royal icing. Cover the cake drum around the cake with leftover pink sugarpaste.

3 Stack the 10cm cake on top and secure to the lower tier with royal icing. Trim both cakes and the cake board with pale pink satin ribbon.

4 Prepare the spherical cake following the step-by-step instructions for a large Temari cake (see page 64). Cover the cake with marzipan and white sugarpaste. If you are using a polystyrene dummy instead, cover it with 2 layers of sugarpaste instead of the marzipan.

5 Prepare the round mini cakes and cover with pale pink sugarpaste (see page 32). Trim the base of the cakes with pale pink ribbon.

Cat Run-outs

Make the run-out cats a day in advance to give them enough time to dry.

1 Place small pieces of greaseproof paper over the cat templates (you will need to make 10 cats from the templates). Colour some soft-peak royal icing with black paste colour, fill a piping bag and cut a tiny hole in the tip. Pipe the outline of the cats.

2 Make 400g of royal icing to run-out consistency (see page 35). Place 2 tablespoons of the icing into a bowl and colour it pale pink. Place the rest into another bowl and colour it black. Place each colour into a piping bag: this will be enough to make 10 cats.

3 Snip the tip off the bag of black run-out icing and fill in the outlines of the cats. While the icing is still wet, pipe pink dots onto the black icing. Leave them to dry overnight.

Top Tip

If you are not confident at piping you can make all the cats from modelling paste, as described below.

Cat Cut-outs

1 Roll out some black modelling paste thinly. Using the same cat templates as before, cut out 12 cats with a sharp knife or craft knife.

2 Stick all the cats around the sides of the cakes with a small amount of edible glue.

3 Prepare some soft-peak, pink royal icing in a piping bag. Snip the tip off and pipe dots onto the cats.

Birdcage

Make the top decoration for the birdcage a day in advance.

1 Roll some black modelling paste into a long sausage shape. Using a smoother to roll over the paste, make 4 x 10cm long, 5mm diameter strips. Curl both ends as shown and allow to dry overnight.

2 Repeat step 1 to roll a long, thin sausage of paste and make a circle for the handle. Allow to dry.

3 Make the 2 bird templates from thin card. Roll out some black modelling paste thinly and cut out the birds with a sharp knife or craft knife.

4 Using a medium paintbrush, paint a tree branch on the surface of the cake with Jet Black paste food colour mixed with clear spirit. Stick the 2 birds onto the cake with edible glue.

5 Roll out some black modelling paste thinly and cut 10cm long, 4mm wide strips using a sharp knife and ruler. You will need 16 strips altogether.

6 Using a paintbrush and a small amount of edible glue, paint lines down the spherical cake where the birdcage pieces will go. Position the paste from the top of the glued line to the bottom and cut off the excess with small palette knife. To neaten the base and hold the cake in place, wrap a long strip of black paste around the base of the cake.

7 Roll a ball from black paste, flatten it and glue it on top of the cage. Secure the dried decorative pieces on top of the cage with royal icing.

8 Once all the pieces have dried completely, place the birdcage on top of the 2-tier cake. Place this onto a stand and arrange the mini cakes on another tier or around the large cakes.

Edibles

Teapot

2 x 15cm (6") dome shaped cakes (for the teapot)*

150g (5¼oz) sugar syrup

400g (14¼oz) filling

600g (1lb 5¼oz) marzipan (SK)

700g (1lb 8¾oz) white sugarpaste

Teacups

6 cupcakes*

6 x 7cm (2¾") half-spheres baked in a silicone baking mould**

50g (1¾oz) sugar syrup

350g (12¼oz) buttercream

450g (1lb) marzipan (SK)

600g (1lb 5¼oz) white sugarpaste

Bulrush, Cyclamen, Daffodil, Gentian and Leaf Green paste food colours (SK)

100g (3½oz) royal icing

1kg (2lb 3¼oz) white modelling paste (made from 500g Sugar Florist Paste and 500g sugarpaste)

Antique Gold metallic lustre food dust (SK)

*Use the 15cm (6") round cake recipe to make 6 cupcakes and 6 x 7cm (2¾") half-spheres.

**Use the 18cm (7") round cake recipe to make the 15cm (6") dome shaped cakes.

Equipment

Large and small circle cutters

6-8 wooden skewers

No. 1.5 piping nozzle

18cm (6") round cake drum

6 saucers (choose a design that you would like to copy)

Melon scoop or small spoon

Cupcake wrappers in your choice of design

> Basic cake covering and decorating essentials (see page 40)

Preparation

Make the handles, spout, base of the cups and saucers a day in advance to allow them to dry hard.

1 Knead 500g of white sugarpaste and 500g of white flower paste together to make modelling paste. Keep any paste that you are not using in a sealed plastic bag to prevent it from drying out.

2 To make the large handle for the teapot you will need to start with 100g of modelling paste. Make a ball shape and gradually roll it into a long sausage. Roll one end to a point and bend it round to form the top of the handle. Adjust the length as required by cutting off the other end then make it pointed and form into a scroll shape. Allow to dry on a piece of foam sponge.

3 Make the small handles for the teacups in the same way from 10g of paste and allow to dry.

4 To make the spout for the teapot, roll 100g of the modelling paste into a ball, gradually form it into teardrop shape then roll it to lengthen the top. Bend into the shape of a spout. Make a straight cut at both ends as shown then let it dry on the foam sponge.

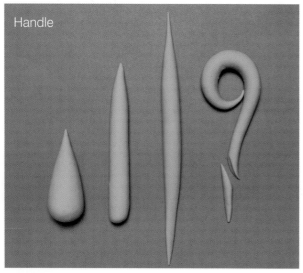

Handle

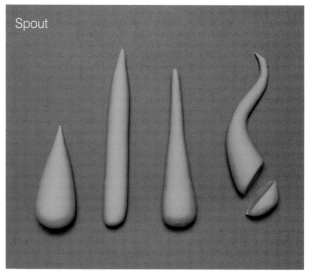

Spout

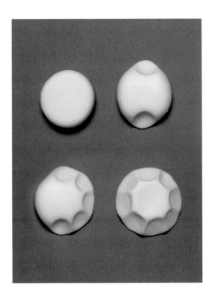

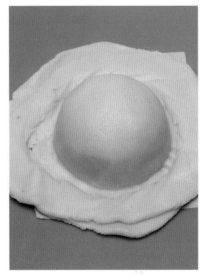

5 For the base of the cups, make a ball from 20g of paste and flatten into a circle. (You can do this with a rolling pin and circle cutter if you find it easier.) Use your fingers to make indentations around the edge. Scoop out a little paste from the centre for the cup to stand on.

6 Colour 250g of paste with a little Gentian or Cyclamen paste colour for the saucers. Roll out the paste to a thickness of about 3mm, using a real saucer as a guide. Roll out the paste further from the centre to make it thinner at the edges. Make 3 saucers in the first colour.

7 Sprinkle some icing sugar over the real saucers and place the sugar saucers on top to form the shape. Trim the edges and allow to firm.

8 Repeat the same method with 250g of paste coloured with a small amount of the other paste food colour to make another 3 saucers.

Teapot Cake

1 Set the cake leveller on the first notch then use this as a guide to cut the ball shaped sponge into slices. Place a piece of cling film into the spherical tin that the cakes were baked in then put the sliced, filled sponges back into the tin (this will help keep the rounded shape of the teapot). Level off the sponge so that it is the same size as the tin. Repeat to make the other half and leave both halves to firm in the fridge.

2 When the cakes are firm, take them out of the tins and use some more filling to stick them together to form a sphere. Slice a tiny piece of cake off to make a flat base and place the cake onto the cake board.

3 Spread some buttercream over the surface of the cake then cover it with marzipan and sugarpaste in the usual way (see page 26). Cover the cake board with white sugarpaste.

4 Stick the handle and spout onto the body of the teapot with some royal icing.

Top Tip

If you are going to transport the cake it is a good idea to support the handle and spout with wooden skewers to hold them securely in place.

5 Colour 100g of sugarpaste the same blue as the saucers and roll it out thinly. Cut out a circle using a large circle cutter or any round object to make a lid to fit the teapot. Make a white ball and stick it on top of the lid with edible glue.

Teacup Cakes

1 Take the centre out of the 6 dome shaped sponge cakes using a melon scoop or small spoon. Fill the holes with sugar syrup and filling. Turn the cakes upside down and cover the surface with buttercream. Leave to firm in the fridge.

2 Roll out some marzipan very thinly and cut out 6 circles slightly larger than the diameter of the teacups. Place the

sponges on the marzipan and cover them with another piece of marzipan. Using your hands and a smoother, form the cup shape and trim off the excess around the base.

3 Repeat step 2 to cover the cups with a thin layer of ice blue and pink coloured sugarpaste.

4 When the cups have firmed slightly, turn them upside down and attach to the base pieces with royal icing. Attach the handles with some royal icing.

Decoration

1 Roll out some white sugarpaste thinly and use the circle cutter set to cut out 6 x 8cm circles for the saucers, 6 x 5cm circles for the cups and 1 x 10cm circle for the teapot.

2 Stick the circles to the centre of the saucers, the top of the teacups and the side of the teapot.

3 Following the step-by-step picture as a guide, paint flower patterns on the teapot and cups using a paintbrush and paste food colours.

4 Prepare some semi-soft peak royal icing with tiny amount of brown and yellow food colours to make a beige colour. Place in a piping bag and pipe a beaded pattern around the edges.

Cupcakes

1 To make the roses, roll out 80g of pink modelling paste into a long, thin strip and cut out 18 rectangles measuring 2cm x 8cm. Roll the paste up into a small bud and pinch it around the edge to get a slightly pleated look. Take off any excess paste at the base. Make 18 roses altogether (3 per cupcake).

2 Using a melon scoop or spoon take out a little of the sponge from the centre of each cupcake. Brush some syrup into the hole, fill with your choice of buttercream filling and spread over the surface of the cake.

3 Colour some sugarpaste with a small amount of Gentian paste food colour. Roll out and cut out a circle of paste with a cutter that is slightly larger than the top of the cake. Place a disc on the top of each cupcake.

4 Prepare some stiff-peak royal icing coloured with Leaf Green paste food colour. Place into a piping bag and cut a V in the tip of the bag.

5 Prepare some soft-peak royal icing coloured pink with Cyclamen paste food colour in another bag. Cut off the tip of the piping bag.

6 Place 3 roses in the centre of each cupcake, secure with the green royal icing and pipe leaves in between the roses. Pipe dots over the top of the cakes with pink royal icing.

7 Place the cupcakes into cupcake wrappers to give them a professional finishing touch.

Damask Design

Snowflake Temari

Sakura Cherry Blossom

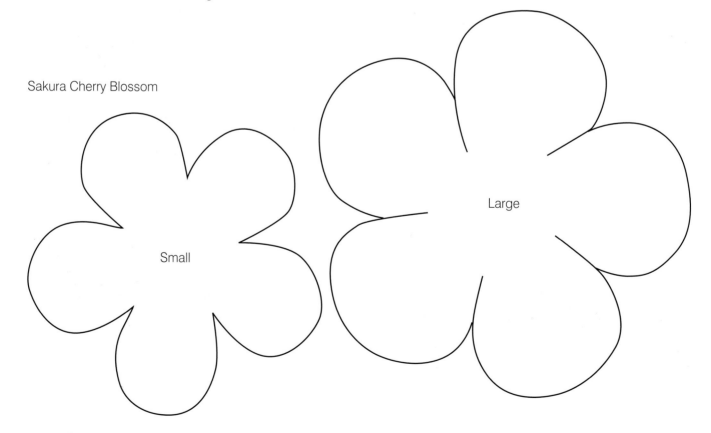

Small

Large

Wedding Bells

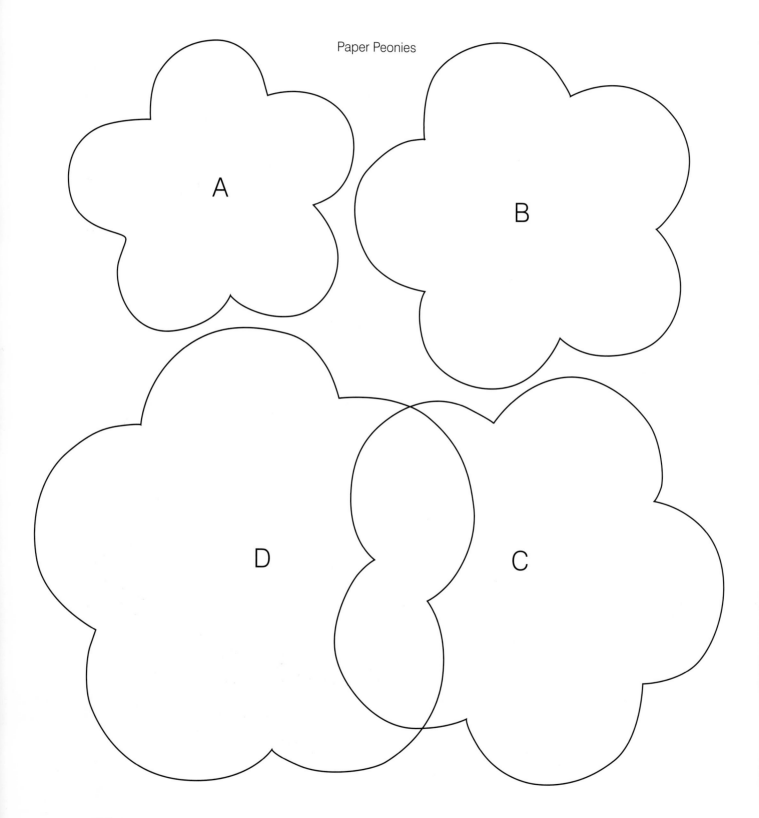

Paper Peonies

A

B

D

C

Templates

Cats and Birds

Suppliers

Squires Kitchen, UK

3 Waverley Lane
Farnham
Surrey
GU9 8BB
0845 61 71 810
+44 1252 260 260
www.squires-shop.com

Squires Kitchen International School
The Grange
Hones Yard
Farnham
Surrey
GU9 8BB
0845 61 71 812
+44 1252 260 262
www.squires-school.co.uk

Squires Kitchen, France
clientele@squires-shop.fr
+33 (0) 1 82 88 01 66
www.squires-shop.fr

Squires Kitchen, Spain
cliente@squires-shop.es
+34 (0) 93 180 7328
www.squires-shop.es

Sugarcraft Shops

Jane Asher Party Cakes
London
www.janeashercakes.com

Blue Ribbons
Surrey
www.blueribbons.co.uk

Cakes 4 Fun
London
www.cakes4fun.co.uk

Catering Complements
Kent
01892 513745

Lawsons Ltd.
Devon
www.lawsonshop.co.uk

The Sugarcraft Emporium
Worcestershire
www.sugarcraftemporium.com

Surbiton Art & Sugarcraft
Surrey
www.surbitonart.co.uk

Sugarcraft Distributors

Guy Paul & Co. Ltd.
Buckinghamshire
www.guypaul.co.uk

Culpitt Ltd.
Northumberland
www.culpitt.com

Manufacturers

Smeg UK Ltd.
www.smeguk.com
www.smegretro.co.uk

Italian appliance manufacturer
Smeg produces distinctive
domestic appliances combining
design, performance and quality.

Flowers

By Appointment Only Design
www.byappointmentonlyde-
sign.com

Flower arrangements for Paper
Peonies and Temari cakes (pages
30 and 64). Handmade cracker
service available.

Vintage Crockery Hire

Pretty Vintage
www.prettyvintage.co.uk
Vintage glass for jam filling
(page 15), and vintage lace table
decoration for Bridal Corsages
(page 44).

Cake Stands

www.re-foundobjects.com

Wallpaper

wallpaperdirect.co.uk
www.interiors-europe.co.uk

Ceramics

**Tougei Mutsuki Ceramic
Studio**, Saitama-shi, Japan
www.h5.dion.ne.jp/~claywork/
Contact: maki@makiscakes.com
Handmade rectangular plates for
Sakura Cookies (page 55).